I0133168

i

Leading Leaders:
Inspiring, Empowering, and
Motivating Teams

Mickey Addison

Blue Mantle Publishing, Inc.
Conyers, GA

Leading Leaders: Inspiring, Empowering, and Motivating Teams

Published by: Blue Mantle Publishing, Inc., Conyers, GA

bluemantlepublishing@gmail.com

This book is available through Lulu.com (search: #13694596) and via Mickey's website at mickeyaddison.com in paperback, ebook, and hard copy. Order forms are also in the back of the book.

DISCLAIMER

The views expressed in this book are those of the author and do not reflect the official policy or position of the United States Air Force, the Department of Defense or the U.S. Government.

Praise for *Leading Leaders*

Colonel Mickey Addison is a leaders' leader. I have personally watched him lead and he practices what he writes about in his excellent book, "Leading Leaders". His book is easy to read and contains leadership pearls of wisdom that the reader can use to become an truly effective leader. The way the book is written and organized makes his principles easy to follow and will enable the reader who aspires to become a great leader, achieve that goal!

- Stephen R. Lorenz , General, USAF (Retired), author of *Lorenz on Leadership*

Our nation is crying out for leaders. In this gem of a book, Colonel Mickey Addison shares the timeless lessons of leadership he learned in sports, in the Boy Scouts, and in a successful career in the US Air Force. Filled with unforgettable stories illustrating the principles of leadership, "Leading Leaders," is a must read for anyone who desires success at the highest level, whether in sports, in business, or personally. Whether you are just beginning your career, or a seasoned executive, you'll want to keep a copy of "Leading Leaders" on your desk as a handy reference. Buy it, read it, and apply its principles.

- Ruben Gonzalez - Four-time Olympian, Author of "The Courage to Succeed" OlympicMotivation.com

Leadership is more than a 9-5 job, and no one lives leadership like the US military. Colonel Addison has lived a life and career of leadership, and he shares his lessons in this great read. Managers of all levels will benefit from this book!"

- Mary C. Kelly, PhD, CDR, US Navy (ret) author of *Master Your World,* ProductiveLeaders.com

Everyone who works on a team or has the role of leading people in any way should read this book. The leadership lessons are valuable for managers, team captains, and leaders from the CEO all the way down.

- Paula Parrish, Director of Development, Our Lady of the Lake University

I've watched Mickey get more done than a single person could ever achieve on their own for nearly two years. Now I see how he does it! Leading Leaders is not only worth the read, but more than that, worth putting into practice.

- Tim Gibson, Brigadier General (sel), USAF

Riveting! A great mixture of personal stories and leadership principles that represent years of Mickey's successful strategies. Perfect for new and long-time leaders; if you only read one leadership book this year, it should be this one.

- Fire Chief Ernst Piercy, Regional Fire Chief at Navy Region Southwest Fleet, Family & Child Programs

Colonel Addison has captured a lifetime of leadership experiences in this elegantly written, and captivating guide. His experiences in inspiring others, grounded in personal character, and refined throughout a distinguished military career, are distilled into this succinct and highly recommended volume.

- Bill Andrews, PhD, Colonel, USAF (Retired), Professor, Eisenhower School, National Defense University, former POW and fighter pilot

Leading Leaders is a must read for aspiring young leaders and serves as a critical reference for senior leaders to gauge their own leadership skills. Mickey captures the timeless foundations of effective leadership through his own experiences as an Air Force officer as well as the successes of those that have gone before him. I look forward to adding it to my library of leadership primers and using it as a reference in my own leadership discussions.

- Todd Salzman, Chief Master Sergeant, USAF (Retired) former USAF Academy Command Chief, Military Relations Manager, Ent Credit Union

More than just another non-fiction work on management or leadership, Addison interjects his own anecdotes throughout the book, and many of them are wonderful examples, not only of successes, but also of failures in communication from which the author has learned much.

- Jeff Koloze, PhD, President, Koloze Consultants

Colonel Mickey Addison has led a number of organizations throughout his life from sports teams to Scout troops to military units. During this time what Mickey repeatedly demonstrated was: while the environment and teammates may have changed, the success he is able to achieve through his leadership process did not. As Mickey so rightly points out, "People change and goals change, but the fundamental leadership challenge of working with a group to achieve a shared goal remains essentially the same." For the executive leader, that means leading other leaders and sometimes "leading" a boss as well. Colonel Addison's experience and success speaks for itself; and his latest book, "Leading Leaders", is a clear and easy to read roadmap showing the way to anyone who is responsible for drawing out the greatness in others.

- Tom Yuhas, VP Sparkle Wash International

"To build something that lasts, you must start with a solid foundation." This well-known adage forms a foundation itself for Leading Leaders. Drawing on his experiences leading people and organizations over a twenty-plus year career as an Air Force officer, Mickey weaves in stories that lend depth and context to the five bricks that comprise his leadership foundation. This foundation works. Sharing a similar background as Mickey, and some of the same senior leaders, I've seen these leadership fundamentals in action around the globe. And I've seen what happens when they're absent. Both aspiring and well-seasoned leaders will put this book down better prepared, or re-grounded, in what it takes to lead successfully.

- Christian Knutson, P.E., PMP, Lt Colonel, USAF, author of "The Engineer Leader" weblog (www.engineerleader.com)

Leadership is so important in every walk of life, but something often elusive to managers. Leadership inspires and creates a situation where people perform collectively and individually at a level far greater than thought possible. This book lays out leadership in a logical format and gives today's managers practical leadership theory, sprinkled with real-world situations of how leadership works...or how the lack of leadership can be destructive. Read this book once as a look at leadership. Read this book again and again as a constant reminder of how to make leadership a part of your management style.

- Sharyn McWhorter, Lt Colonel, USAF (Retired)

"Leading Leaders provides readers with various personal stories from military to civilian that will lead you to principles of building a strong and lasting foundation for leading others and leading "up". The book focuses on human interaction, the leader's character and engagement, and is built on the principles and practical applications of Integrity, Respect, Leaders Lead, Team Work and Little Things Matter. It is a good leadership book for learning how to lead effectively and how to lead leaders."

- Phuong Callaway, PhD, Assistant to Associate Managing Director, National Transportation Safety Board

After working for leaders at all levels and leading large organization myself for nearly 40 years, "Leading Leaders" is the best easily digestible blueprint for being an effective leader I've ever read. Great insight into how to be a true compassionate leader of complex organizations."

- Brian X. Bush, Colonel, US Army (Retired)

This is a tool every leader needs in his/her tool box. Whether you're building a foundation or fine tuning your organization, this is a must read.

- Robyn Sleeth, Deputy Mission Support Commander, US Air Force Academy

As a member of a leadership team of a Fortune 500 company I have attended many "Leadership" training seminars. "Leading Leaders " by Mickey Addison gets to the core principles of what leadership IS and can be applied to any business or enterprise from Little League to the corporate board room.

- Marc Kelly, Tax Manager, CapitalOne

To my brothers and sisters in the service of our Republic, may God protect them, may their causes always be just, and may their leaders always be virtuous.

Acknowledgments

No book is the work of a single author, and I owe this one to a lot of mentors, teammates, and family members who have helped me along the way.

Thanks to my family, led by my wife Betsy, who has endured one re-write and crazy idea after another and who has supported me every step: thank you and I love you!

Thank you also to all my mentors, former commanders, and teammates: Gen(ret) Steve Lorenz, Maj Gen Len Patrick, Maj Gen Tim Byers, Maj Gen Theresa Carter, Brig Gen Brad Spacy, Brig Gen(sel) Tim Gibson, Col(ret) Dave Maharrey, Col(ret) Bill "BA" Andrews, Lt Col(ret) Sharyn McWhorter, Lt Col Pat Carley, CMSgt(ret) Dale Vertz, CMSgt(ret) Ed Dickens, CMSgt(ret) Ed Lubbers, SGM(ret) Dennis and Barbara Watters, Paula Parrish, Brian Bush, Robyn Sleeth, CMSgt Jim Robinson, MSgt Joe Reffner, Olympian Ruben Gonzalez, Dr. Mary Kelly, Rick Olsen,, Marc Kelly, Dr. Jeff Koloze, Dr. Phuong Callaway, Lt Col (ret) Christian Knutson.

Finally, thanks to Maria Johnson and Blue Mantle Publishing for their support and encouragement.

Table of Contents

Preface

I have been privileged to lead a number of organizations throughout my life. From sports teams as team captain and later coach, to Scout troops, to military units during my Air Force career. The environment and teammates change, but my basic approach to leading has not. The fundamental leadership challenge of working with a group to achieve a shared goal remains essentially the same. For leaders at all levels and especially the executive leader, that means leading *other* leaders and sometimes "leading" a boss as well.

To be sure, the leader and the followers have to adapt to each other and the task. The leadership style I used as an executive to lead an experienced senior staff is not the same style that I used when leading a group of teen Scouts. However, any successful style has to recognize the foundational truth that leadership is fundamentally a human problem. This means that leaders have to engage the people they're leading and not treat them as if they were a math problem. We cannot treat people like machines, and we cannot ignore the fact that people have a basic need for affirmation and a sense of fair play.

This book is a distillation of my experience leading people over a lifetime, in sports, Scouts, volunteer work, and, of course, 26 years as an Air Force officer. In fact, I've given the *Leading Leaders* talk every time I've taken charge of a new unit; it's well-practiced and time-tested. It's an approach to developing and leading other leaders based on character and engagement to lay a "foundation" for whatever task the leader to accomplish. This "foundation" has five "bricks" that describe the leader's relationship with the team, the team members' relationships with each other, and the leaders' responsibilities to them.

Leading Leaders is filled with stories about leaders and personal stories from my own life since leadership is inherently a personal experience. Leadership is not the application of skills as much as it's the focused attention on human interaction. Humans are complex beings that are the amalgamation of their own experiences, learned and innate behaviors, and the situations leaders and teams find themselves in over the course of the job at hand. We can learn a lot from our own experiences, and others', so long as we're open to the lesson. That's the real secret of effective leaders: They care enough about the team and the job at hand to invest themselves in the effort. Leaders have to be present and engaged. No effective leader ever "phones it in."

A great story to illustrate my point: I once accompanied an Army two-star general to the signing ceremony of an agreement on enhancing military spouse employment between four military bases in the Rocky Mountain Front Range. It was a typical ceremonial military function, with local officials, base officials from two military Services, and a host of military spouses. As the Army major general made his way through the crowded corridor toward the ballroom, staff in tow, to get ready to start the event, he found himself shaking hands with a volunteer who was also the wife of one of his deployed soldiers. The general could have shaken her hand, smiled perfunctorily, and moved on. No one would have

> *"Obstacles are those frightful things you see when you take your eyes off the goal."*
>
> *- Henry Ford, industrialist and inventor*

blamed him, since he commanded thousands of soldiers and certainly had a full schedule.

But that's not what he did.

He stopped and gave that young woman his full attention. He asked her how she was doing with specific questions and, after listening to her intently, assured her of his support by making certain his aide had her name and her husband's unit. I have no doubt that he checked on her and her husband later, probably personally. It made a huge impression on me to see such focus and presence by a senior leader!

That's presence...that's leadership...and it's applicable to leadership in any situation.

There are many more stories just like that one, and my hope is that you can find a nugget or two in this book to help you make a difference in your work and in your life.

Introduction

Why don't my employees respond to my leadership? Why don't their values align with the organization's values? How do I get my organization to perform at the level I know they're capable?

Those are questions asked often by leaders in every industry and field. Everyone has walked into an office or production floor where morale was low and productivity was lower. Places where pretty, motivational posters on the wall are a source of quiet ridicule rather than inspiration. Places where everyone wears the company logo, but no one embodies the company values. In organizations like that, the most dangerous place is being between the employees and the door at the end of the day.

Powerless managers blame the employees, the generational differences, the economy, or a host of popular excuses, when the *real* problem is likely the leader himself. The truth is that external visuals and artifacts inspire people only when leaders inspire people. Only leaders who understand the relationship between them and their team, and then step up and *lead,* will ever be able to produce high performance in their organizations.

There's an old adage that to build something that lasts, you must start with a solid foundation. I believe the foundation of any excellent organization is an excellent leader or leadership team. Leaders rarely lead teams where they're the only leaders on the team. A football team has an offensive and defensive captain. Military units and large organizations are often organized into hierarchies with leaders at each level. Even small teams have leaders for various parts of the job: this one is in charge of assembly, or that one is in charge of transportation, and so on. I have been lucky to be given leadership opportunities at an early age. Even from those earliest leadership opportunities, I was leading others who had leadership roles of their own beside me and subordinate to me. In Scouts, there was a hierarchy and defined roles among the boys in my patrol. On sports teams and in business there were other team captains and assistant managers. In the military, there have been peer leaders and as I got promoted, subordinate commanders. Leading those people is what this book is about.

Even though I've developed my leadership principles primarily in military and sports environments, I can assure you that *Leading Leaders* principles are universal and can be applied to industry, non-profit, and government. Why? Because good leadership is fundamentally about human interaction, inspiring people to get a job done or overcome obstacles: from combat to craft fairs. Leadership is not a formula or process. There is no product to buy, shirt to wear, or pill to take that can substitute for good leadership, and good leadership requires strength of character from the leader.

One of my heroes, the late Tom Landry, former Dallas Cowboys' head coach, once said that the art of leadership is *"to get people to do what they don't want to do to achieve what they want to achieve."* What Coach Landry understood was the basic leadership dilemma: how to motivate people to accomplish some task, or mission, and to do that in such a way that they get some value out of the deal. That requires leaders who can move people without breaking them in the process.

My view is that the *foundation* of successful leaders, that is, their "character," is the keystone to effectiveness. Character is so

2

basic that, without it, no leader can be successful. The leader's foundation—character—is made up of "bricks"; I'll discuss these in more detail further down.

Before that, however, it's necessary to define "character". Among the many dictionary definitions of "character" was this one from Dictionary.com: "public esteem; reputation." In my mind, this definition is inadequate because, while a leader's reputation is important as an indicator, a leader's character—who they are—is more important. To me, "character" is something within, something that defines a person on the most basic level. I've crafted a definition for character that describes what I'm talking about. My definition goes like this: "character is that which defines a person on the most basic level." In other words, character is who a person truly is as a human being, what he values, and how he approaches life.

President Ronald Reagan sums up the idea of the fundamental nature of character and what it takes to make good decisions as a leader. In a speech to the cadets at The Citadel in South Carolina, Reagan said:

> *The character that takes command in moments of crucial choices has already been determined. It has been determined by a thousand other choices made earlier in seemingly unimportant moments. It has been determined by all the little choices of years past...by all those times when the voice of conscience was at war with the voice of temptation...whispering the lie that it really doesn't matter. It has been determined by all the day-to-day decisions made when life seemed easy and crises seemed far away...the decisions that, piece by piece,*

3

bit by bit, developed habits of discipline or of laziness, habits of self-sacrifice or of self-indulgence, habits of duty and honor and integrity—or dishonor and shame.[1]

In reflecting on this statement from President Reagan, it's important to recognize that he wasn't necessarily speaking about heroes or larger than life figures, although those words could certainly fit the heroes in our midst. He was talking about the common person and the idea that people rarely "rise to the occasion"; rather, most people fall into habits and thought patterns where they're comfortable. That's why seemingly unimportant decisions become the building blocks of character, for good or bad. We have to remember that as leaders we are always "out front."

The people who work with us are unique individuals who have their own web of relationships; their own values; their own desires, ambitions, and values. Once we take on the task of leading people, we have to somehow harmonize their needs with the needs of the group, the organization, and the task at hand. I do that by establishing a common

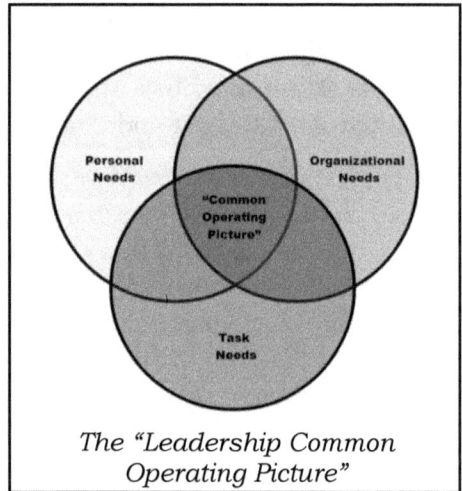

The *"Leadership Common Operating Picture"*

1 President Ronald Reagan, "Keepers of the Peace," Commencement Address at The Citadel, 15 May 1993, accessed 8 Jan 2013, http://www3.citadel.edu/pao/addresses/reagan.htm.

foundation. In the Air Force, that's called a "common operating picture" (COP). The purpose of the "leadership COP" framework is to graphically illustrate the human interactions between teammates and leader and focus those interactions toward the shared goal.

Let me give you an example: a laser beam is a very special light; it's called "coherent light" by scientists and engineers. What makes lasers so powerful is that the light waves are all traveling the same direction. This intensifies the light beam into a laser beam, and the difference is startling. Regular light radiates in all directions. Those lights do a good job of illuminating the room, but if you want the power to cut metal, or even to point something out on a PowerPoint presentation, then you're going to need the focused energy of a laser. That's what good leaders do. Good leaders get all their people, resources, and partners moving in the same direction.

There are lots of ways to do that, but linking the team member's own individual needs to the organizational goals will make success a habit.

Our goals, then, are threefold: (1) understand the relationship between the leader and the follower, (2) understand how ethics and character contribute to high performing teams, and (3) appreciate the "teams within teams" concept of organizational leadership. I've developed five principles that give leaders and their teams a foundation from which to operate; a springboard for organizations to reach their goals and aspirations. The leader's character, the foundation of leadership, is composed of five elements, or "bricks," that, assembled from that foundation, a leader can use to get his team to the next level. The "bricks" in this solid foundation are (1) Integrity, (2) Respect, (3) Leaders Lead, (4) Teamwork, and (5) Little Things Matter.

By mapping leadership goals to these "bricks" in the foundation of leadership, we arrive at the path for understanding the *Leading Leaders* approach. Each of the "bricks" in the foundation directly supports the leader's goals of leading people to achieve. With these five "bricks," a leader can build a solid foundation that will make poor organizations good and high-performing organizations great.

Concept Map – Goals to Principles

Leadership Goal	"Bricks"
Understand the relationship between the leader and the follower	Respect Leaders Lead
Understand that ethics and character contribute to high performing teams	Integrity Little Things Matter
Appreciate the "teams within teams" concept of organizational leadership	Teamwork

6

Cornerstone: Brick One: Integrity

Character may be manifested in the great moments, but it is made in the small ones.

\- Sir Winston Churchill

Integrity First: Honor Codes and Ethics

If we're to inspire people to follow us, integrity must be the cornerstone of who we are. That's why the first "brick" in the foundation is **Integrity**. It is a prerequisite for any success, because, without it, we cannot hope to build the trust of our superiors, establish and maintain relationships, or gain the respect of our teammates. The word "integrity" itself comes from the same root word as "integrated," from the Latin word *integritatem,* meaning "soundness, wholeness, blameless." From the definition, you get a sense that to have "integrity" means you are not divided, not *duplicitous,* not "two faced." What you see is what you get.

Organizations like the Boy Scouts, sports teams, the military, and other highly successful institutions demand and therefore teach integrity as a matter of course. To inculcate integrity, organizations create systems of ethics, and the individual's integrity is measured against that ethic. It often takes training or an indoctrination period for a person to fully understand the ethic of the particular group, which is why many institutions have an "orientation" or training period for new people. Though there are many different systems, there are some basic similarities in most systems of ethics, however, that are instructive.

Honor Codes, and other codes of conduct/ethics are the "systematization" of the principle of Integrity. They provide a written structure for virtue and a touchstone for all members of the community that provides, at best, a guide star for behavior and, at worst, the threat of *dishonor* for violators. The concept of "honor" is relevant to all institutions, not just those with written ethics codes, because inherent in any system is the underlying assumption that people should behave honorably.

For example, at my alma mater, Texas A&M University, there is an honor code: *"Aggies will not lie, cheat, or steal, nor tolerate those who do."* All Aggies, both military cadets and civilian students alike, bind themselves to those words when they accept membership in the institution. Like most, it is an honor system run by the students and guided by the faculty that enforces the rules, but at its core the Aggie Code of Honor is a charge the student accepts when he or she becomes an Aggie. Of course, Texas A&M is not the only institution with an honor code. Every military school and most academic institutions have an honor code with similar words and ideas. As it happens, the Aggies borrowed theirs from the West Point Honor Code (*"A cadet will not lie, cheat, steal, or tolerate those who do."*), as did the Air Force Academy (*"We will not lie, steal, or cheat, nor tolerate among us anyone who does."*) All these institutions have a similar formulation because they have a common ancestry, and similar institutional goals: to produce officers for the military and leaders for society.

The Naval Academy has a somewhat more expansive expression of what they expect from their midshipmen:

> *Midshipmen are persons of integrity:*
> *We stand for that which is right.*
> *We tell the truth and ensure that the full truth is known.*
> *We do not lie.*
> *We embrace fairness in all actions. We ensure that work submitted as their own is their own, and that assistance received from any source is authorized and properly documented. We do not cheat.*

We respect the property of others and ensure that others are able to benefit from the use of their own property. We do not steal.[2]

While the preceding examples are all military schools, it's not just military colleges that have honor codes and standards of behavior. Princeton University's honor code is one of the oldest and is intended as a guarantor of academic integrity. Princeton's honor code, like that of the military schools, was constructed by students. The honor pledge students include on their work is different depending on the work; for example, the pledge for exams is: *"I pledge my honor that I have not violated the honor code during this examination."*[3] This is a written statement, but it need not be a formal written statement in order to be effective.

At Virginia Tech, the Undergraduate Honor System states that accepting membership in the University community means the student accepts the "fundamental beliefs" reflected in the Honor Code:

1. That trust in a person is a positive force in making that person worthy of trust,

2. That every student has the right to live in an academic environment that is free from the injustices caused by any form of intellectual dishonesty, and

3. That the honesty and integrity of all members of the university community contribute to its quest for truth.[4]

2 "US Naval Academy Honor Concept," accessed 17 Dec 2012, http://www.usna.edu/honorconcept.htm.
3 Princeton Student Guide, accessed 17 Dec 2012, http://www.princeton.edu/studentguide/academics_101/honor_code.
4 Virginia Tech University Undergraduate Honor System, accessed 17 Dec 2012, http://www.honorsystem.vt.edu/?q=node/4.

I like several things about this particular formulation. First, there is a positive statement about who the community expects the student to be, namely *a person worthy of trust*. I also like the notion that the honesty and integrity of each individual contributes to the honesty and integrity of the community. These are important points, because while an honor code or ethic regulates individual behavior, it does so for the benefit of both the individual and the community.

Like institutions, professions also have Codes of Conduct and Codes of Professional Ethics that are intended as touchstones for members of their particular professions. Engineers have ethical codes meant to engender the public's trust in their skill (e.g. *"Hold paramount the safety, health, and welfare of the public"[5]*). Physicians' ethics are guided by various versions of the Hippocratic Oath (*"I will apply, for the benefit of the sick, all measures which are required, avoiding those twin traps of overtreatment and therapeutic nihilism."[6]*). These codes of ethics

> *Codes of ethics are ancient. The Hippocratic Oath was instituted in Greece by the Classical physician Hippocrates in the 5th Century B.C. The oath has gone through numerous revisions over the centuries and is voluntary for most physicians as they begin their careers.*

---

5   National Society of Professional Engineers, Code of Ethics, accessed 26 Oct 2012, http://www.nspe.org/Ethics/CodeofEthics/index.html.

6   Johns Hopkins University, Hippocratic Oath (Modern Version), accessed 26 Oct 2012, http://guides.library.jhu.edu/content.php?pid=23699&sid=190964.

serve the same purpose as honor codes that they provide an external "north star" to orient organizational behavior.

All these codes and oaths have several things in common. First, a new entrant to the community takes the group's ethics upon themselves voluntarily, but once taken, they are enforced by the community and the individual. No one forces a young man or woman to accept enrollment to a military college, just as no one forces a young woman through medical school. The honor codes and oaths are taken freely, even eagerly, as a condition to become an officer or a doctor. The point is that members of each community has decided for himself what ethics each thinks are important, and each bind himself or herself to that ethic *on their honor.*

Second, the entrant to the new community accepts the *responsibility* of the ethic that is essentially self-policing. While there are honor courts and ethics review boards, ultimately when a person takes an oath to have integrity, very often the offender is the only one that knows whether or not that oath has been violated. I often use sports metaphors for life, probably because as a Texan "sports" was so much a part of my life. That caveat notwithstanding, there is a great deal to be learned from sport because just the term "sportsmanship" conjures a certain view of how people should behave. We expect athletes to be people of character, and that's why we're so let down when we find out someone has cheated. It's the reason that his sport's governing body stripped Lance Armstrong of his titles. This also is one reason I love sports movies: They usually portray people striving to be the best they can, fairly and with strength of character. In the 2000 Robert Redford film, *The Legend of Bagger Vance* (based on the novel by Steven Pressfield), there is a quote that exemplifies this culture of the personal responsibility to accept the "honor code" of the sport. Hardy Greaves, the boy-narrator of the story, explains why he believes golf is the "greatest game there is" and, in doing so, makes a statement about character [**emphasis** mine]:

> *It's hard and you stand out there on that green, green grass, and it's just you and the ball and* **there ain't nobody to beat up on but yourself;** *just like Mister Newnan keeps hittin' himself with the golf club every time he gets angry. He's broken his toe three times on account of it.* **It's the only game I know that you can call a penalty on yourself, if you're honest, which most people are.** *There just ain't no other game like it.*

What Hardy Greaves understands is that no matter what the rules are, no matter what the enforcement mechanism is, when it comes down to "an integrity check," it's almost always solely the person making the decision and his conscience that are only ones present for the judgment call. No matter who else may be in the room, integrity is always a voluntary decision.

Internal Compass, External Orientation

Adherence to systems of ethics demands an internal compass oriented on an external fixed point. This is very important, because without some external orientation for the internal compass, many people will rationalize almost any behavior. We begin using words like *honor* and *duty*. We examine a person's behavior based on *honesty* and *truthfulness*. Perhaps most importantly, we do not allow a person to "re-define" themselves or his behavior out of following the ethics they accepted. In short, we know very well what the meaning of "is" is.

Ultimately, that's what honor codes and professional ethics do for the individual and the community: They provide a "north star" to orient ethical decision making. Each person experiences life from their own perspective, and if left open to each person's private interpretation uninformed by an external reference, ethical decisions can vary greatly from person to person. Someone who has the view that "all's fair in love and war" and applies that to the business world is potentially opening themselves to behavior that could be unethical at best or illegal at worst. Conversely, an overly scrupulous person could be too timid to take reasonable risks to expand her business or promote her people out of fear of crossing an imaginary line.

> *"You might as well praise a man for not robbing a bank as to praise him for playing by the rules."*
>
> *- Champion Professional Golfer Bobby Jones*

Consider the briefing I once received from a pre-school director. She informed me matter-of-factly and very sincerely that we were "not allowed" to call their annual Thanksgiving meal for the kids a "Thanksgiving Meal" because it was "religious." When I asked who had made that decision and why, she told me that years ago another director had renamed their annual event a "Fall Festival" to avoid offending anyone. The person who made the original decision clearly had her heart in the right place, but her good intentions led her to censor the actual legal name for the federal (and secular) holiday, "Thanksgiving," out of concern that it might offend someone's religious or cultural sensibility. In fact, no one had complained, and no one in authority above her had mandated changing the name from "Thanksgiving" to "Fall Festival."

Concern for others' sensibilities is a good thing, particularly when it comes to religion or other strongly held beliefs. However, the woman who had insisted on "striking from the rolls" the *name* of a holiday had not accommodated anyone or avoided causing offense; we were still celebrating Thanksgiving after all, just by another name. What the name change had accomplished was to sterilize the work environment. Instead of a superficial gesture, what she really needed to do was address the *real* sensitivities of her staff and customers rather than making what appeared to me to be an empty and superficial gesture. The leader must balance the needs and sensibilities of her community with the necessity to avoid euphemism to "fix" problems that don't exist. There are some, in the Native American tribes primarily, who have difficulty with the origins and symbols of the American holiday of Thanksgiving. A leader should be sympathetic to that if she is in a community that expresses that sensitivity. Nevertheless, leaders propagating euphemisms like "Fall Festival" don't really honor anyone's personal beliefs, and I believe that sort of word substitution only makes everyone feel uncomfortable for not calling something by its real name. Superficial gestures come off as patronizing rather than inclusive and can cause team members to question the leader's integrity and "true" intentions. There is often a fine line between patronization and being sensitive to others. Leaders should do their best to determine where that line is and have the integrity to honor the people they serve with honesty.

A better way to approach a situation like this might be to simply and carefully choose how to celebrate the holiday in a way that is inclusive and honest. Additionally, persons that don't want to participate need to feel free to abstain without judgment from leaders or peers. The leader should be willing to defend that person's nonparticipation if necessary, and to maintain the sense of personal space in an organization. For example, why not engage people who are troubled by the conflict between Native Americans and European settlers to find some meaningful symbols that can be included? Or perhaps, honestly and with respect, inquire about the nature of the difficulty and address the issue directly. This approach treats people with respect and the leader can maintain his/her integrity. Even more than that, it makes employees feel valued as the leader's engagement serves to validate their position, and thus, the employee's own sense of self-worth.

Accommodation and inclusion shouldn't turn into some "cultural superiority contest" but a genuine celebration of the various threads (in this example) of the tapestry of American history. Inclusiveness is necessary for

> *Authentic inclusion respects differences and invites participation on equal footing. Patronizing someone's background and tokenism are transparent and are ultimately counterproductive.*

16

building a great team, and a leader of integrity will understand how to integrate people of the various backgrounds into a team that can excel. In their book, *Reframing Change*, social scientists Jean Kantambu Latting and Jean Ramsey[7] use the terms "Dominant" and "Nondominant" traits to describe how to understand diversity in the workplace (race, religion, cultural background, relationship status, etc.). Latting & Ramsey make the case that leading consciously means understanding where employees are coming from and making appropriate adjustments.

What I believe makes inclusiveness effective is not approaching differences as if they were reasons to patronize "nondominant" characteristics or to suppress "dominant" characteristics. A leader with integrity, one who practices it and demands it, will create an environment where people know they're treated fairly and feel comfortable being themselves. Diluting culture to the point of changing the name of a national holiday appears dishonest, and everyone knows it. It may be a small thing to call the official Thanksgiving celebration a "Fall Festival," but it will be very hard for a leader to prove he is not obfuscating other things if the team believes he's willing to use euphemism for something as simple as the name of a national holiday.

> *Organizational policies usually exist for a reason. It's just as important to understand why a policy exists as it is to follow it. Sometimes it's prudent to violate policy, but the leader must do that with eyes open to the consequences.*

---

7 For a fuller discussion of leading teams with "dominant" versus "nondominant" traits in the workplace, see Jean Kantambu Latting & Jean Ramsey, Reframing Change (Santa Barbara: Prager ABC CLIO, 2009), Chapter 5 "Bridging Differences"

Another example illustrates the other extreme, that of the "ends justify the means" crowd. These people live by the idea that rules are for other people, not for them, and that whatever gets the job done is acceptable behavior. It is customary for a base commanding officer to have his own base newspaper and public affairs office. At a particular small base, the base commander had neither newspaper nor a public affairs office, so he co-opted the magazine that was designed and published as an advertising vehicle for his morale and recreation activities to use as a newspaper. It was plainly against Air Force policy, since the money generated by the servicemembers' patronage at their base morale and recreation activities were to be used to support the morale and recreation fund only. The magazine was funded through those revenues, and should have been used to support the servicemembers' morale and recreation programs only.

However, the officer in question felt that using the magazine as a base paper served the "greater good" and simply ignored the rules. He wrote an editorial in each publication and insisted on various base clubs getting free space to announce their happenings for the month. The publication became a cross between a base newspaper and an advertising magazine, growing the magazine into something more than the policy allowed. Furthermore, the officer began to exercise editorial control over the entire magazine, even going so far as to personally approve fonts, artwork, layouts, and the cover design. What should have been the work of a team of advertising professionals able to "flex" to the needs of the market to reach their customers became a monthly ordeal requiring more paperwork and meetings.

The result was a demoralized staff that felt they either had to cover for their boss and wait him out or report him to the chain of command and risk reprisal. The base commander was well intentioned and had a legitimate need to communicate. However, in this instance, by not using any sort of external orientation for his internal compass, he simply rationalized that the ends justified the means. By seizing control over the editorial process, he made the staff self-conscious about other decisions as well, inducing several staff members to leave and stifling the creativity and initiative of the rest. A micro-manager is dangerous enough, but to attempt to micro-manage creative people is doubly worse because it inhibits the aspect of their work they love the most. This creates an atmosphere of fear and resentment, not to mention reducing productivity.

Further, and more to the point, a leader who believes the "rules don't apply" creates factions within his organization that gravitate to the extremes. One faction will emulate the "ends justify the means" attitude and bend (or break) rules themselves. This could lead, at worst, to gross mistakes that legally endanger the entire enterprise. Perhaps a less experienced employee would commit a crime or serious breach of policy based on the idea that "the boss does this sort of thing all the time, so it must be OK." A more experienced and perhaps less honest employee could be emboldened to break the rules (or the law) based on the idea that "since I've got something on the boss, he can't touch me." A leader of integrity follows the rules and sets the example because it's the right thing to do. A leader cannot bend the rules without expecting his followers to do the same, or alternatively compromise his own integrity. Neither of these outcomes is a formula for long-term success.

Creating a Culture of Integrity

Every job, no matter what that job entails, requires integrity, *and* it is very obvious to everyone when it is present and when it is not. In the military, the work is dangerous and often expensive, and even the most junior Airmen frequently have responsibility for many lives, big dollars, or both. But integrity is not confined to life and death struggles on the battlefield. Sports teams demand integrity and enforce it with discipline on the field. Institutions and private sector companies have "ethics clauses" in the contracts of executives. Codes of conduct, even voluntary ones, demand integrity of employees at almost every successful company.

If you handle money, or important information, or someone's or some institution's reputation, integrity is expected behavior. Once one's integrity has been compromised, it's very difficult to get back. It's often said that the measure of a person's integrity is how willing they are to do the right thing even when no one is around. But I believe creating a culture of integrity is more than just "doing the right thing" when you can't get caught. Integrity means *wanting* to do the right thing *because* it's the right thing. Lying, cheating, and stealing: these are breaches of trust and respect. Of course, those behaviors must not be tolerated by anyone, least of all the leader. But he must exhort the team to do the right thing because it's the best course of action for everyone.

> *Never underestimate the power of personal example. People respond to a leader who's engaged personally.*

To create a culture of integrity, a leader must *always* set the example. This is a maxim of leadership at every level and in every walk of life. It is impossible for a leader to demand integrity from her team if she's unwilling to have integrity herself. I'm sure almost everyone has worked for a demanding boss. Sometimes those demands are driven by the nature of the work; sometimes they're driven by the nature of the boss. No one who's been in the workforce very long is a stranger to hard work or a sense of mission, but I hope everyone would agree that even the most unpleasant job is bearable when you know you can trust your boss and teammates.

The leader's character *must* be beyond reproach and unquestioned. A breach of integrity is like mildew: It may not be obvious at first, but it doesn't take long to make the whole place stink. A person may not compromise their integrity because their boss does, but when integrity doesn't come from the top first, the team will rapidly sort itself into factions based on who is "on the boss' side" and who is "not part of the team." Even the slightest breach of integrity by even a single person, and a leader especially, compromises the whole team.

Sometimes even a *perception* of a personal breach of integrity can be enough to demoralize the rank and file. Leaders must manage perceptions of their behavior as carefully as their actual behavior. For example, take the (fictional) case of Mr. Top Guy, the CEO of Top Guy Enterprises. Mr. Guy is an outgoing and friendly man, devoted to his family and very successful. Mr. Guy also loves to mentor young up-and-comers, seeing it as his responsibility to help the young executives to reach their full potential. Because he's busy, he usually does his mentoring sessions over lunch. Mr. Guy's mentees to date have all been men, and he's taken them to lunch at the local pub. The pub offers privacy for discussions in booths, apart from the raucous lunch crowd. But now Mr. Guy has taken on his new project: a pretty young woman named Miss Smith. So, here is Mr. Guy, big shot CEO, taking a woman half his age to lunch.

In this case, Mr. Guy has some decisions to make. He would be wrong not to take on Miss Smith as a mentee and certainly would be wrong not to treat her to lunch like his other mentees, but he probably should choose another venue for the mentoring sessions, perhaps even inviting his wife or another female executive to join them. Mr. Guy has to be aware of his and Miss Smith's reputations, and he must guard both carefully. Further, when Mr. Guy makes a change to how he mentors his subordinates, he should make that change permanent. It is counterproductive to make a change to guard someone's reputation only to be perceived as treating people differently because of their gender.

Because of the way that a breach of integrity by one infects the entire organization, it's very important for the leader to set and enforce standards. A personal failure by a single person, left unaddressed, begins to fester. Other members of the team will wonder if the offender is getting special treatment or perhaps if the offender "has something" on the leader that is preventing them from acting. A lack of action against a breach of integrity lowers both the team's esteem for the leader and the team members' respect for each other. In short, people's imaginations will begin to run wild, and the rumors will often be much worse than the truth. Once a story begins to spread, it

> *Leaders must guard against "the boss said" syndrome. Be careful of off-handed remarks, and be certain subordinates know the difference between brainstorming and orders to do something.*

22

will be difficult to contain, and even when the truth comes out, it may not be enough to re-unify the team. A single incident where a breach of integrity is allowed to fester could take years to recover from, and it may only be recoverable with a change in leadership. The team has to have confidence that they all understand the rules and that everyone is held accountable to those rules uniformly. Somewhat counter-intuitively, I maintain that the principle of setting and enforcing standards actually means *more* freedom for everyone. When everyone understands the rules and believes that the rules apply uniformly, there is a sense of security that allows people to be themselves.

A good illustration of how this principle works is to draw a parallel between rules and Earth's gravity. Just like institutional rules, we could easily say that gravity holds us down, but that's a narrow view. In truth, because of the "Law of Gravity" we are free to move all around the Earth knowing that we won't be flung off the planet into space. What's more, by understanding the "Law of Gravity," humans are able to leave Earth

> *Be careful about which perks you accept as a leader. There is a fine line between accepting earned privileges and becoming unapproachable.*

and navigate through the cosmos. The freedom we enjoy on the Earth is a freedom based in the "known." We all know the rules, and we know that except for fictional superheroes, we all have to abide by the same gravity. There's comfort in that for the people of the Earth. Imagine what a strange and uncomfortable place our planet would be if we had to guess from day-to-day whether gravity would apply to us, or what we would weigh, or even if we'd be flung off into space in our sleep. This is why the maxim that "discipline is good for morale" is true. When people understand and accept the rules, they are free to be themselves and even take risks. The leaders must respect their team and the institution they serve enough to set standards and enforce them uniformly.

I think Winston Churchill's words at the beginning of the chapter summarize that idea: If I cannot trust my boss or my teammates not to steal my Coca-Cola out of the fridge, how can I trust them to manage my office or my funds? How about safeguarding my reputation or the reputation of my institution? On the other hand, if someone is careful with our belongings and respects our reputation, doesn't that indicate they can be trusted with bigger things? Doesn't the entire team function more effectively when we all know we can trust each other?

I've been privileged to work with and for a number of very fine people. Most companies and institutions are staffed with quality people. However, any sufficiently large organization will occasionally spawn what I call the "privilege personality." Unfortunately, I've worked for a few of these people too. This is the person who thinks that their position or authority enables them to lord their success over others, that the company "owes" them their perks, and that the staff exists to serve their personal needs. They believe they've somehow inherited their position in the organization through the Divine Right of Kings, and therefore the entire staff exists to submit to their every personal whim.

This behavior gives the staff license for lack of integrity in return. Human nature will get the best of all but the most virtuous. The staff will cease to show initiative, they will start to do the bare minimum, they will wait for direction, and they will give the "privilege personality" *exactly* what he asks for, no more and no less. The leader ceases to be a leader and becomes a dictator instead, or alternatively, abdicates their responsibility to lead altogether.

Organizations where a "dictator leader" is in a key or senior position are headed for a cliff. Either the company will start to bleed personnel as they head off for greener pastures, or it will bleed money because the staff is no longer invested in ensuring the company is profitable. Something has to give, and either the leader fails or the organization fails. On rare occasions, there is success (usually in spite of the leader) but at such a cost that success is impossible to replicate.

When I was on the inspector general's staff for an Air Force major command, we traveled around from base to base to check the readiness of various units. We did this through what the Air Force calls an "operational readiness inspection," which was three to four days of war games designed to evaluate the unit's ability to fight. When we arrived at one base for an inspection, we found a unit whose morale was the lowest I'd ever seen. They were downcast, they looked exhausted, and they had lost all enthusiasm. It was clear to me their motivation level was "zero," and they were simply going through the motions.

The commander of that unit had made it clear to us through his behavior that his subordinates were there to serve him, not the country. Oh, he never said that explicitly, and if you'd asked him, I'm certain he would have made a speech about duty and excellence. I also believe the commander would've been sincere in expressing his intent. However, actions

> *Senior leaders can never fully foresee the extent their personal leadership style will have on the larger organization. Guard your words and actions carefully.*

25

always speak louder than words. He expected his unit to make him look good, to tend to his personal needs, to like all his ideas…well, you get the gist. What was worse, his people knew it. They knew that the inspection was all about the commander and not about them, the mission, or the unit. Their sense of duty and professionalism carried them, but to be sure, the effectiveness of the entire unit of 2,000 people was compromised.

What happened to this unit during the inspection? Well, they passed, but just barely. The Airmen in that unit were performing out of a personal sense of duty and rote memorization rather than being motivated by their wing leadership. They had not been inspired to *excellence*. Why? Because they were not respected as professionals, and they were not respected as people. They knew their commander lacked integrity, and that lack of trust between the leader and the team manifested itself in mediocre performance and very poor morale. Their commander had violated one of the core ethics of military life: that we serve the country and each other rather than ourselves. Do you think that base was a great place to work? Did the commander leave the organization better than he had found it? No, and the fact is it took years after the commander in question had moved on to repair the damage he'd done to that unit and those people. They had been "taught" not to trust their leader, and that is a toxic lesson. What's more, they had carried that lesson to other units. We all learn leadership lessons from people we follow, and in this case, it was a negative lesson.

Honest Evaluations and Pushing Limits

In every business, no matter what the sector or mission, teams are often asked to take on tasks that are very difficult or even perceived as "impossible." Every business person wants to please the customer, every director in a public institution wants to push his/her team to best serve their constituency, but leaders must not allow their teams to over-promise and under-perform. Leaders need to be clear and honest about what their teams can do, how quickly they can do it, and how much it will cost. There is a fine line between pushing a team past their perceived limits in order to achieve excellence, and pushing a team past their *ability* limits to the point that they cannot deliver.

In order for the leader to know the difference, she has to encourage her team to be honest about their abilities and talents. In return, the leader must be honest with their team in their appraisals. It does no one any good for the leader to give a substandard employee a glowing appraisal because that employee may someday be required to live up to the praise and be found wanting. Further, that employee cannot fix what's wrong in his performance if he is constantly being told he is doing everything right. Again, integrity demands that appraisals be consistently applied to all employees. Different jobs and levels of responsibility will clearly require different standards of evaluation. I'd never attempt to hold an intern to the same standard I hold executives, but the leader should use the same intellectual framework for both. For example, I expect the same level of honesty, effort, and loyalty from the intern that I expect from the executive. I cannot give the executive a "pass" for being abusive to her secretary because she has more responsibility and is under more pressure any more than

I can allow the intern to "pop off" because he is young. Both are held to the same standard.

Regular, honest feedback, informal or formal, is absolutely essential for highly performing teams to maintain (or increase) their performance. I'm not suggesting evaluators be cruel—a little kindness goes a long way—but I am suggesting that employee feedback can't be sugar-coated if the evaluator expects the employee to improve. Whenever I do performance feedback, either for an individual or a team, I try to ensure that I'm providing honest commentary of the employee's performance based on the objective criteria in their performance plan or job description. By addressing performance against the measures the employee knows and has presumably accepted, the feedback session doesn't become about the *person*; it remains focused on performance. I have had too many feedback sessions with my boss in the past where I'm told, "You're doing great; don't change a thing!" This sort of feedback is useless, and I believe it isn't honest. No one is perfect, and like everyone, I have room for improvement.[8]

> *Employee feedback has to be honest and focused on making them better at their jobs. There's no room for personal agendas.*

Honest evaluation has to go both ways. If a leader is unwilling to listen to feedback from the team, it undermines his or her integrity. I suppose there are organizations out there with leaders who are brilliant and need no feedback to perform at very high levels, but I've never seen one. In my experience, the leader

---

8 A sample employee feedback form utilizing these principles is located at Appendix 2.

has to rely on honest feedback from his teams to constantly reassess his approach and goals. The leader must be sure that he or she can take feedback as well as give it; otherwise they run the risk of appearing arrogant. No one likes a Know-It-All. In the end, it's up to the leader to lead the team to reaching the goals they've set, but the leader doesn't do it alone. Whenever I give feedback, I always allow the "ratee" to provide feedback to me as well. It offers them an opportunity to clarify things, and I've learned a few things about my leadership style that I've adjusted over the years by asking and being open to what my subordinates were willing to tell me. Blind spots in a person's demeanor are called that for a reason, and sometimes it takes a brave subordinate to point out that his boss is not being effective. In short, ask questions and be willing to accept the answers.

The more senior the leader, the less likely he is to receive honest feedback from his subordinates. Whether or not the team adores or despises their leader, people will often hold back criticism and mute disagreement. This makes the task of eliminating blind spots more difficult as leaders become more senior in the organization. It also means that when a leader, particularly a senior one, finds a person who is willing to give honest feedback, he should cultivate that relationship and reward the behavior. Each time I took on a new leadership position, I had to quickly learn who had the courage to tell me the unvarnished truth and who did not. New subordinates have to learn to trust their leader, and the leader has to learn who he can trust with what information. I find the best technique for ensuring I receive, and continue to receive, honest feedback is to avoid putting subordinates into a position where they're asked to provide me direct adverse feedback in public. Invite subordinates to speak in private so you are their only audience. No one wants to be perceived as a "suck up," so protecting the relationship ensures the subordinate has the freedom to continue to give counsel.

A word of caution is also warranted here: the more senior the leader, the more the imperative that he spread his attention around among his subordinates. Informal authority at executive levels is often as important (if not more) than formal authority. In order to preserve relationships with the entire staff, leaders absolutely need to avoid even the appearance of favoritism. People will naturally develop friendships, and a personal confidant will certainly have more access to an executive than other subordinates, but the senior leader absolutely must reward performance on the same standard for all those who report to him. Senior staff has to know that they will be rewarded based on meeting the leaders' expectations and not based on how much they "suck up." This serves at least two purposes. First it enables the staff of senior leaders the freedom to communicate candidly among themselves and with leadership. Second, it preserves the integrity of the institution by measuring everyone by the same yardstick (performance) rather than by their relationship with the leader.

Only by understanding the team both at a group and personal level, their strengths and weaknesses, can the leader hope to ensure high performance. Integrity in behavior, evaluation, and feedback is vital to that sort of organizational awareness. It allows the leader to know how far a team can go and how capable they really are. A well-led team will strive to reach their full potential

> *Honest feedback is vital to improved performance, but be sure you guard the ratee's pride. Always address behavior, not the person, and above all be kind.*

and even exceed expectations, whereas a poorly led one will fail more often than not. It's all about how honest we are with one another *before* the stress of the current task hits the organization. A poorly led organization will crack under pressure, while a well-led one will thrive on the same test.

To accomplish our goals, be they personal or corporate, integrity must be the hallmark of our creed as leaders. There *must* be trust in the organization, because to fail in the integrity department is to fail in the job and in life. Finally, the leader must always remember that "it ain't about you." Leadership is challenging, rewarding, and even fun; but it's also a responsibility. When leaders make their position all about themselves, they're doomed to failure. Once the leader understands their job is to lead and inspire others rather than be served, the more effective they'll be in achieving their goals. It follows then that the institution and people they lead will also see the fruits of that success.

Moral Courage

Most of us will never lead troops in combat or run into a burning building to save someone, so physical courage is not something that will ordinarily be required of us. *Moral* courage, however, is required of everyone daily. Daily decisions about how to do our jobs and live our lives form us into the kind of people that we are. Individual decisions certainly have more or less weight in importance, but nonetheless they contribute to our character. Do we do the inspection or merely sign off on the form? Perform the inventory or just guess at how much is there? Do we take time to do a proper performance review for our employees, or do we just have coffee and "call it even"?

Poor decisions can aggregate into poor performance. Not doing an inspection of a piece of equipment may mean that we miss a safety issue that could be dangerous. Failing to count the number of widgets on the shelf could lead to lost sales, or worse, someone being falsely accused of theft. A leader who fails to do proper employee feedback could inadvertently encourage bad behavior by subordinates.

> *It is curious that physical courage should be so common in the world and moral courage so rare.*
>
> *- Mark Twain*

Moral courage is more than just following company policy; it's also having the courage to act in a situation where there's injustice. In 2013 Michael Garcia, a waiter at a Houston restaurant, refused to serve a customer who he felt was being disrespectful to a special needs child at another table.[9] It was a risk because his boss could've fired him, but Mr. Garcia believed he was standing up for a person who was unable to stand up for himself. The customers left the restaurant, and the special needs child's family wasn't even aware of the exchange. But when the story did get out, Mr. Garcia became a hero to that family and to the families of special needs kids around the country. In the process, the restaurant got some free publicity, and the city of Houston got an example of how to concretely demonstrate respect.

A few weeks later, another employee didn't get the same response as Mr. Garcia, demonstrating why it sometimes takes courage to act. Twyla DeVito of Shelby, Ohio, watched a regular patron and board member at the American Legion post where she worked get into a car appearing to her to be drunk. Unable to prevent the man from driving away, she called the police.[10] She was subsequently fired by the Post Commander for her actions. DeVito defended her actions by saying, "If he had gotten in a wreck that would have been on me, because it was on my shift...I chose to possibly save a life." I'm certainly not going to second guess either her decision or her boss', but the entire situation serves to illustrate that sometimes there are no "good" decisions; there are only "least worst" decisions. Ms. DeVito had the moral courage to follow her convictions and do what she thought was right.

9 "Houston waiter refuses to serve customer who insulted Down syndrome boy," Foxnews.com, 20 Jan 13, accessed 9 Mar 13, http://www.foxnews.com/us/2013/01/19/houston-waiter-refuses-to-serve-customer-who-insulted-down-syndrome-boy/

10 "Ohio Bartender Fired After Calling Police on Drunken Driver," Rachel Katz, ABC.com. 28 Feb 13, accessed 9 Mar 13, http://abcnews.go.com/blogs/headlines/2013/02/ohio-bartender-fired-for-calling-police-on-drunken-driver/

Opportunities to demonstrate moral courage often come from our boss's expectations. Sometimes there is pressure from a superior to do something unethical, like falsifying records or lying to a customer. Leaders need to remember that while there will sometimes be adverse consequences

> *Pennies do not come from Heaven. They have to be earned here on Earth.*
>
> *- Margaret Thatcher*

for making the right call, there will always be consequences for unethical decisions. It takes a great deal of courage to stand up to a boss. In the best possible case, a diplomatic subordinate can walk a boss back from an unethical decision by explaining the consequences of the poor choice and offering a better one. In a worse case, a person may have to be prepared to risk their employment to maintain their integrity.

Most often the pressure to make unethical choices comes from peers. The excuses are well worn: "Everybody is doing it," "No one will know," "It's only pennies," etc. It takes a special kind of moral courage to walk the line between estrangement of one's co-workers and compromise of one's ethics. It's easy for leaders to be blind to these types of pressures on their employees. Leaders are often busy, and employees will naturally keep amongst themselves those things they don't want to show their boss. Leaders bear a responsibility in these situations to set the example and make sure employees know they can approach him with information of unethical choices by the team. This underscores the necessity for leaders to be engaged, to know their people, and to recognize when they are under stress.

When a leader recognizes his employees are pressuring one another to make unethical choices, he has a responsibility to intervene. There are a variety of ways to do this, ranging from the very impersonal public announcement ("I've become aware...") to very personal private meetings to discuss the matter individually with all involved. Only an engaged leader can know what method to use, and that engagement only comes when leaders have invested the time in relationships.

For the employee who's under pressure to violate her conscience, it can be a hard situation to endure. Sometimes there is no clear solution: Not everyone can afford to quit her job, and moral people aren't willing to compromise their integrity. A situation like that may mean estrangement from teammates or even the boss. Moral courage is even more necessary in a scenario like that, because an ethical person will have to endure pressure from all quarters. That's why we call it moral *courage* and not merely moral strength. Courage requires commitment and usually comes from a storehouse that's hard to deplete, while strength can eventually run out. The courage required to continue to come to work in an environment where one's values aren't respected is not for the faint of heart. That sort of moral courage requires a person to reach into a repository built up over a lifetime, but it's worth it in the end. Just like Hardy Greaves' description of golf, we have to be strong enough to be true to our own values, particularly when working in an environment that's hostile to those values. You're the only one who can call a penalty on yourself in those environments, because your co-workers surely won't do it. When the end of the workday comes, a person still has to live with himself, and being able to do that is worth the effort to develop the strength of character required.

Chapter Take-Aways

- A breach of integrity is like mildew: If left un-cleaned, it will soon make the whole place stink.

- The leader must set the example. Leaders cannot expect a higher standard of behavior than they exhibit themselves.

- While integrity is a personal trait that rests on a person's individual conscience, that conscience must be informed and aligned to an external orientation.

- Company codes of conduct and ethics must be consistently applied to all employees.

- Honest evaluation and feedback are crucial to high performing teams and a culture of integrity.

Questions for Discussion:

1. If you were to write a personal "honor code" or "code of ethics," what would it look like?

2. Choose a "hero" you know personally. What about their personality was most attractive? Why?

3. What does the term "integrity" mean to you?

4. Have you ever been on the receiving end of someone else's breach of integrity? How did it affect you? How would you have handled that situation differently?

5. How do you provide feedback to those you evaluate? How does it focus on objective criteria? Do you ever provide feedback to your boss? How?

Brick Two: Respect

You can easily judge the character of others by how they treat those who can do nothing for them or to them.

~ Malcolm Forbes

The Leader Creates the Climate of Respect

The second brick in the foundation of leadership that's necessary when leading leaders is **respect**. The leader must model respect and demand it of their teams.

Respect must go both ways, up as well as down, and most of the burden falls on the leader's shoulders. Respect is both inherent, and it is earned. It is earned by the way we do our jobs, the way we treat others, and how we carry ourselves. Just as important, respect for the organization is a necessary component. Respect is also inherent in each person as a matter of simple human dignity.

It is very important for a leader to *explicitly* outline his or her expectations in this regard. Everyone should expect their co-workers and their leaders to follow the law, that's a given. Our attitudes about the people we work with should convey that our *hearts* as well as our *heads* demonstrate our respect. The leader must also pledge that they will show respect to their team. A person who shows respect to others will create a

> *Make your expectations about employee behavior and organizational goals known on the first day in a new position, then reinforce those expectations often.*

"bubble of trust" around them. People will *want* to work with them and for them. Customers will *want* to do business with them. The more people in an organization that have built their reputations on mutual respect, the bigger that "bubble of trust" grows. When people know they're respected by their teammates and leaders, they feel safe to perform, to take risks, and to be themselves.

Whenever I took command of a new unit, I made it very clear that we were to respect each other as Airmen and as persons. For us, that meant we used proper military customs and courtesies, we didn't use foul language, and we respected each others' dignity whether or not we agreed with our teammates' choices or beliefs. Each person has a multitude of ways to describe them: sex, race, eye color, religion or no religion, national origin, etc. We are required by law to treat people equally in all things and not to treat someone differently because they are different from us. It's not necessary for me to agree with everything another person thinks or believes, but it is necessary for me to treat them with the respect they deserve as a fellow human being.

In the private sector, this is no different. Like the public sector, there are institutional policies and public law that require certain personal and institutional behaviors, but *respect* is not a legal requirement. Respect is much more than that. Beyond mere adherence to the law, respect is recognizing that another human being has the same value as I do because they *are*, not because of what they *do*, how much money they make, or what clothes they wear. Now, I can certainly perform rote behaviors and parrot legal scripts when dealing with others, but to truly show *respect*, that has to come from the heart. Again, I don't have to condone behavior or agree with beliefs that don't match my own; but the skilled leader, the effective leader, separates *behavior* from *personhood* and can show respect to anyone regardless of

> *"The secret of success is sincerity. Once you can fake that you've got it made."*
>
> *- Jean Giraudoux French diplomat, dramatist, & novelist (1882 - 1944)*
>
> *Despite what Jean Giraudoux says, you can't fake sincerity.*

differences. This type of respect engenders respect in return. Over the course of my career, I've led and worked with a number of people who were very different from me. Because we lived and worked in an environment where respect was the expected behavior, teams and friendships usually form quickly, even among very dissimilar people. We became friends with people we might never have even met, let alone socialized with, because the climate our leaders created and maintained *required* that we respect each other. When you start with respect for another person, most times the differences don't really matter all that much.

> *Bad news never gets better with age. Be sure you are the sort of person employees know that they can bring bad news to you and that you'll act.*

Of course, there are some things in the "just don't do it" category, for example: sexual harassment, alcohol abuse, illegal drug use, racism, etc. These are inherently self-destructive behaviors that leaders cannot tolerate under any circumstances and go well beyond mere "philosophical differences." In professions like heavy industry, construction, the military, police, or fire service, these sorts of self-destructive behaviors can have life or death consequences. In business, it can end careers and destroy companies. Leaders have to act quickly to prevent someone's illegal choices from costing someone else their life or livelihood. In industrial settings, the consequences for the "just don't do it" behaviors are similarly severe. However, not all of us work in a life and death profession. So while leaders in an office or small business may not have to deal with an industrial accident, business and personal consequences can be very severe. Moreover, an incidence of sexual harassment damages the victim and could expose the firm to legal action for not addressing the illegal behavior.

How many teams have been rendered ineffective because of the boorish (and perhaps illegal) behavior of one person? There have been a number of high profile scandals in the last ten years, where leaders failed to act on information that criminal acts were taking place in their organization.

The 2012 Penn State scandal is instructive because, as these sorts of scandals go, it has a lot in common with the many other scandals in large organizations. Look at the personal and institutional wreckage caused by the systemic failure of a handful of people to report the criminal abuse of minors by Jerry Sandusky. For decades while at Penn State, Mr. Sandusky preyed on young boys, and at some point his co-workers and leadership began to believe something was amiss. However, instead of leaders forcefully and directly addressing the situation by asking some basic questions (or better, reporting the matter to the authorities), it appears that Sandusky's behavior was swept under the rug.

Even when Sandusky was caught in the act of abusing a boy in the locker room by a coach, and the matter was reported up the chain of command, the Administration took no action other than telling Sandusky not to bring children to the Penn State locker rooms any more. That wasn't the only time someone observed Sandusky's behavior during the 15 years the grand jury investigated. According to the grand jury investigation, at least 21 people in leadership positions, some of them executive leadership positions, had first-hand knowledge of the abuse and didn't act. The institution suffered far more damage than it would have had the leaders had the fortitude and integrity to confront Sandusky and contact the authorities. More tragically, their failure to swiftly address the situation to the proper authorities not only tarnished the reputation of the institution but enabled a serial abuser to continue his destruction of young lives far longer than he should have. The victims and their families will have a long road to recovery, and the personal wreckage is tragic beyond words.

Leaders have to do the hard work of holding to personal, professional, and legal standards. To do otherwise doesn't merely endanger personal reputation of the offender; it endangers the entire enterprise. It will be years, perhaps even decades, before Penn State recovers its reputation and self-respect. For the foreseeable future, the thousands of current students, faculty, and alumni will have to live with the stain caused by a very small number of people. They will also have to live with the permanent damage done to the victims by someone the University had celebrated as a hero and role model.

I think the response by student body and alumni should give leaders pause when they believe they're protecting an institution by hiding wrong-doing. After the initial shock wore off, the students and alumni demanded accountability. They petitioned for the resignation (or removal) of the University president and demanded that the statue of former head football coach Joe Paterno be removed. They raised money for the victims of sexual abuse to the tune of $574,000. In the end, after all the emotion and grief over the scandal, the majority

Former Penn State Head Coach "Joe Pa" Paterno ended up being dismissed by the University Administration prior to his retirement with his 61-year legend permanently stained. Sandusky is serving at least 30 years in a Pennsylvania prison.

44

of the students and alumni accepted the punishments meted out by the authorities and sought to do their best to reclaim their honor. It was the best they could do to salvage a horrible situation, but it was a failure of integrity by leaders that made a horrible situation much, much worse.

Teach New Team Members

The culture of respect that leaders create must be cultivated and maintained. No team stays static in its composition, so leaders at all levels have to be ready to bring in new members and teach them the organizational culture. It does no good to establish a good company culture and then have it gradually eroded as new people arrive without adopting the values the leader has worked so hard to establish. Furthermore, a leader should always be on the lookout for fresh talent so that his team doesn't stagnate but continues to grow. Nothing stunts a highly performing team faster than stopping recruitment. Without new ideas and perspectives, even the most robust organization withers.

Every large organization has a "new employee orientation" program of some sort. Some of them are a few hours or days; others are weeks long. If all that occurs during these orientation sessions is getting the new employee into the pay and personnel system, then companies are missing the boat. Every organization, be it five or five thousand, has a culture and values the leader expects people to espouse. The true value of an orientation session is to provide the employee with the motivation to accept and internalize the mission and values of the company. If the only time anyone ever talks about the purpose and values of the company is when they look at the wall art, then leadership is lacking.

The military does a very deliberate job of indoctrination of new recruits into the culture. A shared sense of mission and belonging by its members is one of the reasons the military is successful, and its "graduates" are in high demand by employers. These shared values are deliberately introduced and cultivated throughout training to gain servicemembers' personal commitment to the military mission and their chosen branch of service. Arriving

46

at their first duty station, the training continues. They learn the heritage and honors of their own unit, they learn to revere the artifacts of that unit (e.g., its flag and insignia), and they are taught to believe their unit is the finest anywhere. The culture of service and excellence is reinforced: The new recruit is expected to wear the uniform in a certain way, to show respect for officers and non-commissioned officers, and to meet exacting standards of behavior. The culmination of all these culture-shaping behaviors is a group of individuals who think and act as one, particularly under stress. The organization does not remain static, new recruits enter constantly, and leadership changes up from time to time as well. As new members are brought in to replace others who have left the unit, they also assimilate the Service and unit culture. New recruits bring with them new perspectives and new ideas, all the while accepting the values of the organization they are joining.

While civil organizations are not expected to take up arms for their country, this same sort of system can be used very effectively in the private sector. When new employees enter into an organization, take the time to share the company mission and values with them. Explain why taking on these values is beneficial to both the individual and the group as a whole. Civilian companies need not require the same haircuts and clothing, but some sort of unifying "uniform" is useful for creating a sense of unity among the team. It can be as elaborate as a uniform and as simple as a standard nametag. Company values should be talked about and visible. Many companies have their mission and values on display in the entrance of the workspace so that employees see them whenever they enter or leave. Further, the *customers* also see said values, so employees know that they're not just expected to behave in a certain way around the boss.

Most importantly, organizational leaders must embody the values they espouse. If the company says it is about "fair dealing," then it must be fair with employees as well as customers. If the organization espouses "transparency and accountability," the leaders can't skip the annual audit. This is the very best way to motivate employees to adopt the company values: leaders walking the talk. Putting the core values on the wall is one thing, but those in authority have to be willing to demonstrate that they find value in adopting those values by living them.

I remember one time, when I was in college, I borrowed my friend's new Ford F150 pickup truck and promptly dented the driver's side door. I was mortified. I took the truck to the dealership, and the service manager ended up going over the dent with me. As he examined the door, he ran across a manufacturing defect in the door seal. In those days, Ford Motor Company's motto and ethos was "Quality Is Job 1." He ran his hand across the defect, and as he did, he quipped, "Job 1." Then he followed with, "We'll fix that too, while I have it in, no charge." It impressed me, because this man obviously understood that the company's values should be his values. "Quality Is Job 1" was more than just an advertising slogan. For him, it was a way of doing business with integrity. You can be sure that his service personnel felt the same way. They were following a manager who not only believed in what he was doing, but he lived it out.

Setting the example is powerful, and it works.

> *Ford Motor Company is one of the United States' most prolific and successful automakers. The first Ford Model T rolled off the assembly lines in 1903. Today Ford is an international company that sold 4.6 million cars to Americans in 2010.*

Honest Mistakes Are OK, But Crimes Are Not

A culture of trust and respect means that people need to be allowed an honest mistake from time to time. "Allowed an honest mistake" doesn't mean that there are no consequences for making that mistake; it means that there is a difference between a mistake and a crime. The main difference, of course, between the consequences of a mistake and a crime is that the boss often has a choice over how hard to "come down" on someone for a mistake. A crime is a different matter and must *always* be dealt with by the law enforcement authorities. No one should get a pass for a crime.

There's a scene in one of my favorite mini-series, Tom Hanks' *From the Earth to the Moon,* that I think illustrates the difference between accepting mistakes and crimes. During testing, Grumman engineers were trying in vain to understand why the legs of the moon landing ship kept buckling. It turns out that an engineer had made a math error in his initial calculations for the leg design that had carried

> *"Results! Why man, I have gotten a lot of results. I know several thousand things that won't work."*
>
> *- Thomas Edison, inventor and entrepreneur*

through the rest of his work. The project fell months behind schedule and millions of dollars over budget. After spending all night working to discover the error, the young engineer in charge of the leg design sheepishly approached his CEO the next morning and confessed the error was his. Believing he was to be fired, he offered to go home. Instead, his boss scolded him gently for having made the mistake and then thanked him for bringing the matter to him. The CEO then told his depressed and exhausted engineer to get some rest because he had a lot of work to do to get the project back on schedule. The engineer was held responsible for his failure, but the boss also realized that the work his team was engaged in required innovation and risk taking. No one had been injured, and although the company had expended considerable resources, it was not a total loss. More importantly, if every error were a "mortal sin," then the chilling effect on the rest of the team would stifle creativity and reduce the chance for successfully landing a man on the moon. He had to create and maintain an environment where the individual team members knew they were valued and respected not only for their contributions but because they were valued as people.

Of course, the United States landed men on the moon and returned them safely to the Earth using the vehicle designed by that same Grumman engineer who made the initial mistake. That success was made possible because the climate of respect among teammates was strong enough that an employee could approach his boss and confess a mistake, even expecting to lose his job, without fear of being mistreated. An institutional climate where people know they are valued because they *are* creates an atmosphere that breeds excellence.

Grow Your Leaders

Leaders have to *grow their company's future leaders*, because even those with natural leadership ability need training and mentoring. This means that branch managers, assistant managers, team leaders, project managers, etc., have to deliberately develop their teammates' and employees' leadership skills by giving them opportunities to lead and then *letting them.* Give people the opportunity to excel, give them the tools to be successful, and then guide them to success. This idea of setting people up for success and then getting out of the way means that leaders have to be willing to allow their mentees to fail. Sometimes the personal and professional growth from a failure is greater than from success.

The 10th Contracting Squadron is the organization responsible for all procurement at the Air Force Academy, and they do between $200–300 million in acquisitions each year. They buy everything from supplies to construction to complex cooperative agreements with industry to support Academy research. Their training program is a superb example of how to deliberately develop and grow personnel into future leaders. The Director hires a large number of interns, many with no acquisition experience. He plans for formal institutional education for his new employees, but development doesn't end there; he has an internal continuing education program, where the interns meet for lunch to discuss their projects, listen to guest speakers, and ask questions of more seasoned

> "Well, you can't never let *anything* happen to him. Then nothing would ever happen to him. Not much fun for little Harpo."
>
> - *Dory, from Pixar's* Finding Nemo

employees. Additionally, there is a consciously monitored program by senior leaders, where new employees are mentored, given increasing responsibility, and allowed to make decisions (and mistakes). The real "trick" to developing employees into leaders is the understanding of what mistakes are necessary for the greater good of growing future leaders in the company and what mistakes need to be avoided. Yes, mistakes are sometimes necessary. That's often how people learn, then those in charge have to allow their teams to try new things and, at least occasionally, make a mistake. The worst error a leader can make is not to allow employees to make errors. Conversely, the best investment in the company a leader can make is to develop employees that will grow into the future leaders in the company.

Eventually, everyone moves on, and if leaders truly care about the organization they're a part of, then they'll ensure they've done what they can to hire and develop quality people to replace them when the time comes.

Be A Leader Worthy of Respect

For a leader to be successful, he or she must engender the respect of their subordinates. As I've mentioned earlier, the tyrant rarely reigns very long. The leader should expect to be respected, even demand it, but he must be worthy of that respect if it means anything. Anyone can be bullied into respecting someone's rank or position, but it takes a real leader to engender the respect of their subordinates.

I was member of the Corps of Cadets at Texas A&M, a military organization of 2,000 cadets embedded in a major university of 40,000 students. As freshmen, we were at the very bottom of the hierarchy, voluntarily surrendering our rights and having them doled back out to us as privileges. But once each year the freshmen were given the chance to switch places with our upperclassmen. For one day, we would be cadet corporals; we would have authority over the same upperclassmen that had been training us all semester. We schemed, we planned, and we couldn't wait to get even. After all, we were going to wear *corporal's stripes!*

If the leader merely requires protocol without earning respect, then the protocol becomes a reason for ridicule. Earn respect by demonstrating respect to peers and subordinates.

We soon found out that stripes (and yelling) don't make a leader. Our subordinates-for-the-day were unwilling to grant us any authority based on the temporary stripes and certainly not based on the volume of our voices or the urgency of our demands for respect. Our best laid plans disintegrated before our eyes into an unruly, undisciplined, and chaotic mob of "freshmen" who refused to obey even the simplest commands.

By the end of the day, we'd learned that respect is never given or worn on our collars. Our upperclassmen gathered us together to explain the purpose of the day's events: We should not expect to be respected merely by changing our rank insignia. We had to *earn* the respect of our followers by treating them fairly, communicating clearly, and following the rules. Furthermore, our upperclassmen had taught us that the high standards they expected of us were worth it. We had witnessed first-hand an "example" of low standards, and we were repulsed by it. The next year, as sophomores, we put these lessons to the test as squad leaders for the new "fish" (freshmen) in our unit, and we ended up helping to create a culture of a very high performing unit.

A very tragic event that occurred in the first weeks of our sophomore year underscored the leadership lessons we'd received during our freshman year. Our upperclassmen had impressed upon us the necessity to model the behavior we required of our own freshmen, and it paid off when the "traditional" methods of discipline were removed from our leadership "toolbox" after a sophomore cadet died in a training accident. Unable to simply have our freshmen "drop and give me 20 pushups" when they transgressed the rules, we had to find more subtle and non-physical ways to enforce the standards. As a squad leader I learned that a low steady voice is much more effective than a shout, and leading by example got better results than constant correction. The Corps weathered the storm and was better for it in the end, but those leadership lessons had come at a very high price.

My cadet squadron continued to perform exceptionally well. We even won the Corps academic award, which had been a goal of our cadet squadron since its inception two years before. I attribute this performance to our upperclassmen, the Classes of '85 and '86, instilling in us the desire to excel while all the while setting the example for us to follow.

Respect for the Institution

There is one final aspect of respect and that is respect for the institution to which one belongs. The leader must demand that respect, and model it through his own behavior. Just like any other breach of respect, a lack of respect to the institution where a person works is cancerous. If allowed to grow, that lack of respect can kill the body. In short, if you can't respect the institution, then get another institution.

Respect for the institution looks very similar to respect between individuals, and like an interpersonal relationship, it cannot be forced. And just like an interpersonal relationship, deeds are more important than words. All the fancy logos and motivational posters cannot make up for treating people fairly and having transparent human resources policies. People must have confidence that the organization where they work is a place where they feel valued, and a place where they are respected. Their workplace as an organization must be a place where "HR" is not a dirty word!

> *Respect for the institution is just as important as respect for between teammates. If employees don't respect their company, it's likely they won't respect the company's customers or their own fellows. That's a recipe for a very unhappy and unproductive work environment.*

In the best possible case, people will take on the organization's values because those values are something to which they want to aspire. Companies get a reputation for being great places to work for a number of reasons but usually boil down to things like fair compensation, the ability for managers to be flexible, and empowering employees to make decisions about their careers. It goes without saying that when employees find value in the company's mission, they find more value in their individual role in that mission.

For example, according to *CNN Money Magazine*, the top three companies to work for in 2012 were Google, Boston Consulting Group (BCG), and SAS Institute[11]. Employees at all three companies reported they felt valued by leadership, their work was meaningful, their pay was good, and that the workplace was a fun place to work. Google's success as an organization is legendary: good pay, self-paced work, and plenty of free food. BCG has a focus on work–life balance, including requiring their employees to take time off, which demonstrates they value their employees' well being as much as they value their productivity[12]. SAS has a number of programs emphasizing the value of their employees' well-being, including subsidized Montessori childcare, intramural sports leagues, and unlimited sick time.[13] All three of these companies value their employees and prove that through their HR policies. What's more, the leaders themselves model the behavior they require of their employees.

According to a 2012 Gallup survey on employee well being, the most important factor in how employees felt about their job was their level of engagement. "Engaged employees," those who

---

11 "100 Best Companies to Work For, 2012," CNN/Money Online, 6 Feb 2012, accessed 15 Nov 2012, http://money.cnn.com/magazines/fortune/best-companies/2012/full_list/.

12 Leslie A. Perlow and Jessica L. Porter, "Making Time Off Predictable—and Required," Harvard Business Review, October 2009, page 4.

13 "100 Best Companies to Work For, 2012: 3. SAS Institute," CNN/Money Online, 6 Feb 2012, accessed 15 Nov 2012, http://money.cnn.com/magazines/fortune/best-companies/2012/snapshots/3.html.

work with "passion and feel a connection to their company," was the group who scored highest on wellbeing. In *Harvard Business Review*, Jennifer Robison reports:

> [The study authors] *weren't surprised to find higher levels of wellbeing among engaged employees. Nor were they surprised to find that engaged workers were substantially more likely to say that their employer offers "a lot" or "some" flextime -- or that engaged employees work slightly more hours than do their actively disengaged or not engaged counterparts.*[14]

I think before employees can become "engaged," they have to believe they're valued and respected by the institution and their co-workers. How does a leader engender respect for the institution? Lots of companies have perks and good pay, but the companies listed above have managed to engender the respect of their employees by creating an environment where the perks and pay were *indicators* of the respect and value the company placed on its employees rather than a cold transaction. The perks and pay themselves don't matter as much as the way they're delivered. No

> *While you can't be your employees' friends, you can be a friend to them. Understand your employees' goals and dreams and help them achieve them. Doing so will pay dividends in work environment harmony and productivity.*

---

14   Jennifer Robison, "For Employee Wellbeing, Engagement Trumps Time Off," Gallup Business Journal, Online, accessed 3 Jan 13, http://businessjournal.gallup.com/content/159374/employee-wellbeing-engagement-trumps-time-off.aspx

matter how high the pay is and how much free food a company hands out, if the employees believe they are being bribed or bought, they will not feel valued. An employee who believes he are not valued won't perform and probably won't stay.

The leader creates an environment of respect by first and foremost respecting the members of his team. Leaders must treat their subordinates with respect, both in demeanor and in compensation, before any of the team will be willing to return that respect to others or the institution. Aside from the usual and expected signs of respect and common courtesy, the *effective* leader goes further: They appreciate that the time spent at work or on task is not the sum total of their employees' lives and treat them accordingly.

The effective leader understands the personal and professional stressors in his subordinate's lives and takes those stressors into account when assigning tasks or evaluating performance. This is not to say that poor performance is excused. On the contrary, the leader has a responsibility to hold team members accountable for their performance. But understanding the "why" of an employee's decisions and performance can direct *how* the leader responds to employee performance. For example, if an employee who is struggling with personal difficulty makes modest improvements in his work, that success might be worthy of some recognition. When a leader understands that an employee has overcome some obstacle in his life and managed to be successful in his job as well, a leader can bolster the well being and future performance of that employee with a well-intentioned compliment.

Conversely, if the leader is watching a usually high performing employee's output plummet, then some understanding and even an offer of help can mean the difference between a continued downward spiral and an employee returning to being a productive member of the team. It has never ceased to amaze me how much a kind word of encouragement and direct engagement from a leader motivates employees, and I've seen it work wonders time and time again.

Moreover, the leader who's engaged has a better viewpoint and more information to make decisions on work assignments and evaluation. "Know your people" is the mantra of many military leaders to their subordinate leaders; a mantra based on the idea that the engaged leader is more effective at motivating teams. The engaged and informed leader understands the environment he or she is operating in and makes the

> *"If you are trustworthy and passionate about your cause, you will attract followers. You will become a person of influence, which is what leadership is all about."*
>
> - Ruben Gonzales, Four Time Olympian

necessary adjustments to get the most from the people she is leading. By getting to know their teammates and subordinates beyond the platitudes and perfunctory small talk, leaders can best understand what work assignments best suit certain people and what best motivates each person on the team. Johnny is good at individual projects; Susie is a good informal leader, etc. By playing to the strengths of the *individuals* in the organization, the *team* becomes more effective. The whole becomes greater than the sum of the parts.

Perhaps most importantly, an engaged leader demonstrates to her team that she sees them as human persons with inherent worth rather than being valued only at their level of contribution.

What's more, that leader can ensure that each employee sees his/her work as meaningful, which as Jennifer Robison pointed out in *Harvard Business Review,* employees who see their work as meaningful are far more likely to find satisfaction in their jobs and workplace. In this way, leaders have demonstrated both personally and institutionally that they value their employees.

A final word about the care and feeding of the team. In the military, there is a saying that illustrates how leaders see their roles regarding the care of the people under their charge: *leaders eat last.* What this means is that the leader has to provide for her people before accepting comforts for herself. There are plenty of stories about officers dining in opulence while the troops shiver and eat cold food, but that's largely a Hollywood stereotype with little basis in fact. A good officer or sergeant makes sure his troops are fed before eating themselves. They also share in the suffering of their troops. If it's cold meals out of a bag for the troops, it's cold meals out of a bag for the leader. This behavior demonstrates to the troops that they have value and that the leader himself is committed to their well being and willing to share in the discomfort of even the lowest ranking Airman. If Airmen are going to accept orders that might put them in harm's way, they need to know their officers aren't making those decisions with callous disregard for their safety. It's a matter of trust between the leader and the team.

That translates to the private sector easily: executive or managerial perks should be used sparingly, and the leader should *personally* check on the working conditions of the team. Know if the workplace is too hot or too cold, if the bathrooms are dirty or in poor repair, if the food in the employee cafeteria is lousy or not, or if Mary Smith is exhausted because she's worked a double shift two days in a row. Don't be afraid to send someone home to get some rest or request an employee take a couple days vacation so that she can recharge her batteries. The slight drop in productivity because Mary is allowed to go home early will be made up in spades by a team that knows you're more concerned for *their* well being than *your own*. Those sorts of leaders are the ones people want to work hard for, and that sort of leadership inspires people to give their best.

Chapter Take-Aways

- Leaders have to show respect and demand it from their teams and peers alike.

- Most mistakes are fine; correct them, then move on...but crimes are not. The leader must know the difference and hold the standards.

- Respect is earned through behavior. The old adage, "They don't care how much you know until they know how much you care," is still true.

- Respect the institution or find another institution. Nothing drags a team down faster than someone who doesn't want to be there.

Questions for Discussion

1. What would you change in the climate of your workplace to increase the "respect level"?

2. What traits or characteristics of your institution engender your respect? What would you like to see done differently?

3. How do you respond when a member of your team shows disrespect to another?

4. How do you communicate your expectations about respect, both as legal and moral requirements, to your subordinates and teammates?

Brick Three: Leaders Lead

Dear General McClellan, if you're not going to use the army, may I borrow it for a while?

~ Abraham Lincoln

Take Charge

If you are in a leadership position, then you must take charge and lead. I call this principle, "**Leaders Lead,**" the third brick in the foundation.

Although the term "manager" is a common title in business and public sectors, there is a reason I've chosen the word "leader" throughout this book instead of "manager." We manage *things*, but we lead *people*. When I was a very young second lieutenant, a wise lieutenant colonel

> "When in command, command."
>
> - Admiral Chester W. Nimitz, USN, 1885-1966

named Larry Isaacs reminded me during a performance feedback session that "people are not machines." I have tried never to forget that truth. We can certainly push people, and most people are very willing to work hard when they know they should, but when we cease to see our team as human beings, then we're entering an organizational death spiral. We need to lead people and treat them like people rather than cogs in some machine that produces a product. It doesn't mean that the product is not important. No one is in business to provide a hangout for the employees, but "leading people and managing things" means we understand the difference and don't confuse one for the other. Leading means taking charge and exercising the authority one is given. "Management" is a necessary skill for a leader, but it is not a substitute for leadership.

As I alluded to in the stories from my time in the Aggie Corps, I've learned that leadership is not merely a matter of barking orders or acting "in charge." The leader has to take charge and make decisions. Even in the military, we rarely bark orders. In an emergency or in combat, certainly, but in our routine day to day it's best to ensure your teams understand what they're doing and why. Furthermore, a leader can only "bark" so many times before their team simply tunes out the raised voices. I've seen it plenty of times in sports. Teams that are accustomed to hearing their coach yell and make demonstrations simply stop listening to the coach's histrionics; they're mentally somewhere else when he is speaking. So yelling and demonstrations simply don't work very often and neither does rule by fear. A leader who relies on fear to motivate their employees has a very shallow toolbox. Put another way, if a leader's only motivational method is fear or arm-waving, he won't last very long and probably won't get much accomplished.

In the military, the overarching mission is usually summarized in a statement of "commander's intent": an explicitly defined end state or goal of a particular mission. While one might not use the same words in business or sports, the same principle of clearly stating the objective applies. The effective leader ensures people understand what's required of them, and then she follows up to see the task through to completion. They give their teams a sense of purpose.

Most organizations have more than a single leader. They have "layers of leaders," and the principle of "Leaders Lead" requires that all leaders exercise their authority. Leaders at all levels should show initiative and work together. If a team leader is waiting for direction, then he is essentially waiting for their boss to make a decision for them. That's not leading. Furthermore, a "reluctant" leader will only inspire the informal leaders in the group to begin to vie for power. A vacuum must always be filled; if the leader at any level creates a void through inaction, then someone will usually fill that void. It's a sure bet that the leader won't have his job for very long. Someone will replace him, the company will fail, or the team will disintegrate.

Now before you get the wrong idea, I'm not advocating leaders exceed their authority, but I am suggesting that leaders should exercise the authority that their boss has vested in them. If they work in an environment where integrity is expected, within a culture of respect, then even a hierarchical organization can be very effective. No matter what the organization looks like on paper, ultimately it's the relationships that matter.

Expect High Standards

Each organization in an institution or company has a job to do: Leaders exist to execute their jobs in support of their company's objectives. That means, internal to an organization, leaders should support their bosses and their institutional goals. My experience is that people rise to the leaders' expectations. Set high standards and hold people to them, and all things being equal people will meet them almost every time (conversely, if you set low standards...). Standards must be uniform; everyone knows how counter-productive "teacher's pets" can be. Everyone wants to be successful and wants to feel that sense of accomplishment.

Expecting high standards is more than merely setting high sales goals or demanding perfection in quality. It means that leaders expect and demonstrate high personal and professional standards in the conduct of their lives and business. I don't mean we create a "Stepford company" of robotic overachievers, but we do expect that ethical behavior at work means that we have ethical behavior in our private lives. We serve our cause, institution, and each other best when this is the case. Entrepreneur and co-founder of Medical Imaging Company, combat veteran, and former fighter pilot David Specht once shared his theory about why people fail that I think is very astute: "If someone fails, they usually fail for one of three reasons: either they weren't trained, they weren't resourced, or they weren't led." Dave's view is one I agree with, and it illustrates the responsibility for the leader to lead by investing

> *Expectations must be very clear, but follow through is just as important. "Inspect" what you "expect."*
>
> *("Hat tip" to Admiral Hyman Rickover, USN)*

himself in the team's success. If there is failure, the leader usually has himself to blame, at least initially.

Apart from George Bailey's uncle in the film *It's a Wonderful Life*, it's a rare case indeed where the failure of an employee is *solely* responsible for an organization's failure. However, even if it's the sole employee's fault for a failure, it's the leader's *responsibility* to get the task accomplished. An effective leader accepts responsibility for the failure of the team and diverts praise for success to their teammates and subordinates. It's very unseemly for a leader to try to blame others for the failure of the team, just as it's a morale killer for the team when the leader tries to take the glory for the success. The leader in those cases isn't fooling anyone; everyone knows success is a team effort, and the leader is ultimately accountable for failure. Trying to divert attention only lowers the leader in the esteem of others.

The quote at the beginning of the chapter is a real one, and it is one of my favorite Abraham Lincoln quotes because it is an example of a senior leader's willingness to call a subordinate to account for "decisional paralysis." During the Civil War, the Union army was plagued by a series of ineffective generals. Some were incompetent, others merely timid. During a moment of frustration over General McClellan's reluctance to take the fight to Lee's Rebel Army of Northern Virginia, Lincoln wrote those words. There was considerable tension among the senior generals of the Union Army and the President, and McClellen had no affection for U.S. Grant. In fact, McClellan ended up running for president against his former boss in 1864 (and lost). Lincoln was looking for a leader, someone he could trust to get the job done. The 16th president was willing to replace Union generals until he found one who could do the job: Ulysses S. Grant. As disdainful as Lincoln was of McClellan, he praised Grant because Grant understood what was at stake and was willing to do what was necessary to secure Lincoln's vision of a reunited country. Of Grant, Lincoln also once said, "I can't spare this man, he fights!" That's high praise for a warrior, but more importantly, it demonstrates the trust Lincoln had in Grant to exercise personal initiative, understand the president's intent, and to move out and make decisions. In short, Lincoln could trust him to lead.

Grant's success as a general was not merely in pleasing his boss; he also inspired his troops. The soldiers of Grant's Army of the Potomac understood the value of a general who "fights" as well. After the Battle of the Wilderness, 5-7 May 1864, the Union army was bloodied in an inconclusive three-day battle. The Wilderness was a terrible battle, where soldiers fought in the dense thicket at close range and often hand

U. S. Grant was the fourth General-in-Chief of the Union Army. Lincoln fired the first three either because of personal conflict or perceived incompetence.

to hand. Some even burned to death in the tall grass as the firefight set the tall grass on fire among the fallen and wounded. It was a hellish three days. Sadly, the soldiers had experienced this hell before. After previous bloody and inconclusive battles, the army had formed up on the road, made a left face, and marched back to Washington, D.C., to await another commander and more grand ideas for winning the war. They had become cynical about their generals and had lost their belief in their ability to defeat Lee's Army of Northern Virginia. It was not that they were incapable or cowardly—far from it—but their generals so far had been incompetent and indecisive. The casualties during four years of conflict thus far had yielded nothing but blood and defeat.

But this time, the officers and men of the Army of the Potomac had a leader worthy of their heroism in combat. They formed up on the road like they had always done, but this time they made a *right face* towards the south to pursue Lee's Army. The Union Army's previous poor generalship and political infighting had produced defeats that translated into a myth of Lee's invincibility. Lee and his army were skilled and courageous, but they were not invincible, and the low morale the Union Army suffered prevented the Federals from winning battles even when they outnumbered the Rebels. This time it was different, however. Although the men of the Army of the Potomac had suffered more than 17,000 casualties in bloody fighting, the men actually *cheered* when they turned south. They had known for years they could defeat Lee's army and end the war if given the chance, and they cheered because they finally had a leader who believed in them as well. Such is the power of a leader who is willing to take charge and *lead.*

A Word About Discipline

It's very important to hold people accountable for their actions and to do so fairly and swiftly. That said, discipline can't be the excuse for running a gulag in the workplace. Holding those two ideas in balance is the key to effective workplace discipline and adherence to standards.

In order for a leader to hold people accountable, the rules must be clearly understood by all involved. This is usually done by writing them down in a document like an employee handbook. To be an effective communication tool on workplace standards, however, an employee handbook has to be written in plain language and relatively short. Handing over a 100-page pamphlet with 8-point font and written in legalese will not only ensure the document is never read, it will likely cause the employee to wonder what on earth leadership is thinking. In fact, the employees at a workplace with such a document will probably consider their leaders detached and aloof.

Far better is a simple summary of the "rules of the road" with references for detailed further reading. For example, there are myriad laws and regulations that govern how employers may hire and fire employees. A guide written in plain English with references to the actual law or other source document is far better than trying to reprint all possible laws and regulations; perhaps even a companion website with direct links and an HR

> *Proper planning prevents poor performance.*
>
> *- Royal Air Force maxim*

professional well versed in the laws and company policies that can answer questions should employees have them.

73

With clear and easily understood guidelines, the leader must be prepared to hold employees accountable for poor performance and must address that performance deficiency quickly. There is a right way and a wrong way to address performance failures. The right way is directly, politely, and privately. The wrong way is raised voices and publicly. If the leader takes a condescending tone, the discipline will fall on deaf ears and fail. Remember, the ultimate purpose of discipline is to *rehabilitate the performance of the employee* not change the employee into another person.

Certainly there are employees who cannot or will not meet the standards set by their boss, and they should not be allowed to drag the team down. In my experience, willful poor performance is rare. The willfully substandard employee may be given a chance to change their behavior, but if he is unwilling, then he should be dismissed swiftly. A failing employee may not be in the right job or even the right profession, and the leader doesn't have to sacrifice his team's performance on the altar of an employee's self-esteem. There comes a time when an employer must terminate the employment of one of his subordinates. This should be done fairly, in accordance with the law, and as gently as possible. Persons don't lose their dignity because they are unsuccessful in a given occupation.

Discipline must be swift because it is uncommon that an employee's poor performance goes unnoticed by the rest of the team. The failure of the leaders to address substandard morale drags down the entire team. By quickly dealing with performance problems, the leader reinforces the idea that they are fair and take the standards seriously. People respond to that sort of leadership and respect the leader who upholds the standards. Everyone likes their indulgent uncle, but no one wants to live in his house very long. It quickly becomes chaos when standards aren't enforced, as the team ultimately loses confidence in their leadership. What follows are motivation problems, a lack of respect for each other and the institution, and eventually an "anything goes" mentality that can lead to organizational ruin or worse.

When I was a new parent, my aunt told me a story that reinforced how important it is to set and maintain boundaries. She told me that if you place a child in the middle of a pitch black room and leave him alone, the child will begin to search for the walls. When he finds a wall, he will push on it to test its firmness. If the wall falls over, and if the process repeats itself on each of the walls in the room, then the child will find his way back to the center of the room and remain there, afraid to explore any farther. Without boundaries (represented by the walls), the child loses his sense of security and will "hide" in the middle of the room. If, however, the walls are firm and unmoving when pushed, then the child will play about the room knowing that he is secure. The moral of the story, of course, is to set and enforce standards. In doing so, then our employees will feel secure and able to do what they've been hired to do. Most people are uncomfortable with ambiguity, and a boundary-free environment will create timid employees. An environment with clear cut rules and well-defined boundaries will have the opposite effect and actually encourage employees to innovate!

Spread Out Decisions and Push Out Authority

It is vital for the leader to push decisions to the lowest possible level or risk organizational gridlock. I once worked in a public works department where the director was the only one who could make decisions. He intervened in even the most minor disputes and decisions several layers below his in the organization. The result was predictable: The business of keeping the city's streets clean and the utilities working ground to a halt. When a 400-person department responsible for hundreds of millions of dollars of streets, utilities, and emergency services had to wait for a single person to make all but the most mundane decisions, the branch and division leaders ceased to lead or even think ahead. They waited for guidance, and they discouraged new ideas that would require them to get the director's approval. The workers on the "line," who actually performed much of the work, "turning wrenches" as we said, began to resent their foremen and branch chiefs for their apparent inability or unwillingness to make even simple decisions. Soon there was discord and grumbling, followed quickly by the best of the staff either retiring or moving on to other work. Eventually, the director had a very significant personal and professional failure that caused him to be removed, but it took years for that organization to recover their pride and their productivity.

In the preceding example, it was a public sector organization in crisis, so profit was not an organizational motivation, but can you imagine what would have happened to a company that's in business to make money? The productivity in that public works department was very low; we were likely *costing* the city more money than we would otherwise have had we been well led. Had we been in business, we'd have priced ourselves out of the market quickly. A "Leaders Lead" organization is one that distributes authority and empowers leaders to make decisions.

So what does an organization that spreads out decisions look like? It doesn't have to be "flat" or without structure to be effective at pushing out authority. In fact, many hierarchical organizations like the military, large corporations, and sports teams are very effective at empowering leaders at all levels, while holding those leaders accountable for their decisions. Successful leaders set clear goals, communicate them to their subordinates, and ensure those goals align with their bosses' goals. The boss then ensures their subordinates have what they need to accomplish those goals. Want to see an organization that innovates, that expands and grows, and that accomplishes the goals the executives set for them? Then give subordinate

> *"Aggies never lose; sometimes we get outscored and we run out of time, but we never lose."*
>
> *- Texas Aggie saying*

leaders the tools and turn them loose. If those leaders don't perform, assuming they've had all they needed to succeed, then the executives have to reassess either the goals, the tools, or the personnel. Accountability goes hand in hand with empowerment.

Google is a fabulous example of this principle. The leaders at Google empower their employees to do self-directed projects on company time with the idea that eventually their effort will pay off for the company. So long as the leader-directed projects are getting done on schedule, the employee and even teams are free to expand Google's list of applications and features. Google calls this approach "Innovation Time Off," and the company encourages their engineers to spend 20% (!!) of their time working on projects that interest them. Google apps like Gmail, GoogleNews, and AdSense are examples of apps that made it into the Google product line because leaders empowered employees to innovate and take risks. AdSense is now one of Google's most lucrative products, earning $9.71 billion (28% of Google's total income) in 2011.[15] That would seem a very good return on the company's investment in affording their employees "Innovation Time Off."

15 Google Investor Relations, online, "Google Announces First Quarter 2011 Results," http://investor.google.com/earnings/2011/Q1google_earnings.html, accessed 8 Feb 13

First Line Leaders Get It Done

It does no good for the CEO to sell a grandiose vision if the VPs and team leaders aren't buying. Furthermore, if first line and mid-level leaders are undermining the CEO's vision, then the ensuing lack of respect for the institution begins to break down the team just as surely as if the leader had a personal breach of integrity. It falls on those same first line supervisors to implement the CEO's vision and to do it in such a way as to communicate the enthusiasm the CEO himself has for the endeavor. The difference between an mediocre organization and an excellent organization is often these first line leaders' commitment to the company vision. That commitment is measured in how that first line leader can translate the task he or she's been given with sufficient enthusiasm to get the employees motivated to excellence.

That's why the military spends so much effort to develop their first line leaders. We depend on sergeants to give the orders that get their soldiers moving. They must understand the commander's objective so well that they can make it simple for their small group and then improvise on the fly if necessary.

> *Investing in first line leaders has an enormous return on investment. First line leaders are most responsible to motivate employees and make daily decisions. Good ones can make the company a lot of money.*

The same is true in business. The team leaders and assistant managers must understand the boss' agenda and then sell that to the employees *as if it were their own idea.* It is counter-productive for the assistant manager to stand up at the beginning of a shift and announce in monotone that "corporate has decided that we'll...."

79

Employees have already stopped listening. What that assistant manager has to do is tell his team the "what and why" and motivate them to achieve both for their own fulfillment and to achieve the company's goals.

It's also incumbent upon leaders at all levels not to merely "sell" the company line but to understand as best as possible the reason their boss came to the decision they did. This is a very important point. First line leaders have the most responsibility to motivate and train the people who actually do the company's work. "Because I said so" has a finite lifespan and becomes very tiresome when used too often. The company leadership should arm first line leaders with the "why" so they can tell their teams. Employee morale and effectiveness starts at the team leader level; employees who rarely or never learn the "why" will soon believe they are unappreciated. Once the downward spiral of morale begins, it's difficult for even the most talented leaders to rescue it. Executives owe it to their company leaders to ensure that they not only understand the task but also understand the why. Not every first line leader will agree with decisions made above them, but if she is to pass on the company's direction successfully, she'll need to understand why senior leaders made the decision in the first place.

Be a Good Follower

Following is just as important as leading. To be a good follower means more than merely doing what your boss tells you but trying to see the bigger picture and understand where the boss is going. I maintain that you've got to learn how to follow before you can learn how to lead. So how do you become a good follower?

To begin with, a good follower always works the boss' agenda first and foremost. Even in small teams, it's usually not possible for the team to fully understand the environment where the leader is operating. People go to different meetings, are privy to different levels of information, and have a relationship with their own bosses (*everybody* has a boss). No matter how effective or ineffective a leader is in doing *his* job, the team must

> *"There's a saying around here that you have to learn how to follow before you learn how to lead. Believe me, you follow like hell your freshman year!"*
>
> *- Texas Aggie cadet quoted in Will van Overbeek's "Aggies", Texas Monthly Press, 1982*

continue to do what they've been hired to do to the best of their ability. There are both altruistic and selfish reasons for taking this stand.

Basic self-respect and integrity require an employee to do what he is being paid to do. Admittedly it is no small task to continue to perform if one is working for someone who's either incompetent or abusive, but "slacking" or not performing degrades a person's self-worth and in the end does more harm to the employee than an abusive boss could ever do. I worked for a very abusive boss once, and the experience was probably the worst year of my career. One of the only things that helped me get through that year was the knowledge that I was giving my best effort and that I had done right by the organization. Even though my boss didn't treat me with respect, I had maintained my self-respect because I didn't let my teammates down. It was that continued performance that got me hired away to another job, a promotion of sorts, that accelerated my career. Had I given up and allowed my performance to suffer, I wouldn't have had that opportunity.

The personal reasons are probably more obvious. Everyone has a boss, and if you're performing, eventually your boss's boss will notice. Even if no one in your organization notices, your performance won't go unnoticed by your customers (or even competitors). Always doing your best and demonstrating loyalty to your organization and your boss as a good follower are qualities employers look for when hiring. By working hard for your old boss, you could work yourself into a better position or a promotion.

> *Decisions are never made in a vacuum; understanding the environment is crucial to making good ones. Sharing information when prudent can be the difference between a poor decision and a good one.*

As a leader, you can build good followers by modeling the behavior yourself. For example, when given direction from your boss, pass it on with the same enthusiasm as if it were your own idea. That might take a little acting at times, but if you hold your boss up to ridicule, you'll be opening the door to your subordinates to ridicule *you*. Loyalty is contagious; demonstrate loyalty and you'll engender loyalty in return.

Another way to model good followership is to work your own job as if you were sitting in your boss's seat. By trying to understand your boss's stressors and stakeholders, you can better deliver what your boss expects of you. No one likes to do "re-work," least of all a busy executive. A follower will be much closer to "final" if she constructs the response to a task or builds a product with her boss in mind. Most leaders are busy, and while most try to communicate clearly, no one is a perfect communicator. Actively listening for *context* when your boss assigns a task, then *anticipating* the questions your boss will be asked by their boss, gets the product much closer to final.

Figuratively putting yourself in your boss's seat also has the benefit of training you for the next level of responsibility. Eventually your boss will want to send someone to a meeting in his place, and the person he or she knows understands the environment the best is likely to get the nod. That sort of confidence and exposure can lead to better performance and even personal advancement. Clearly, it's bad form to compete with your boss for his job, and that's not what I'm suggesting. But there are always opportunities for career advancement, and if a leader is committed to developing their subordinates, they won't pass up the chance to recognize and reward talent. Even if that's not the case, being a good follower usually makes the team a better place to work in general. When your boss knows he can count on you, you're much less likely to get micro-managed and much more likely to be successful. Everyone benefits when the leader and team work together smoothly.

Chapter Take-Aways

- As a leader, don't be a single point of failure.

- Deliberately develop leaders in your organization. A resilient organization is one that distributes authority and empowers leaders to make decisions.

- It is vital for the leader to push decisions to the lowest possible level or risk organizational gridlock.

- Resist the urge to make decisions for people. Teach them to show initiative or help them find another position.

- Support the decisions of leaders in your organization. If you need to correct something, do it quietly, but never undermine a leader who's making a sincere effort to do what they were asked to do.

- Develop your follower skills along with your leadership. Everyone has a leader, and modeling good followership is just as important as leadership.

Questions for Discussion

1. What are the "single points of failure" in your organization, and how can they be mitigated or even eliminated?

2. Whom do you follow? What can you do to improve your followership?

3. Is authority centralized or de-centralized in your organization? What are the pros and cons of your organizational decision-making process?

4. What is the disciplinary process in your organization? Is discipline for infractions consistently applied across your organization? If not, what can be done and by whom to improve the process?

5. If you were in charge of your company's leadership development program, what would you do differently?

Brick Four: Teamwork

Learn from others' mistakes...you don't have time to make them all yourself.

~G.K. Chesterton

"We" Is More Powerful Than "I"

In any endeavor, **teamwork** is usually the key to success. Every organization functions as a team; we all need each other to be successful. Whether your company is 5 or 5,000, there are teams of people who have to work together to get the job done. It is a rare task that a person accomplishes on his or her own. This is not to downplay individual achievement, far from it, but the idea that teamwork enables organizations to reach their goals.

Ever watch an interview with a NASCAR driver? From the outside, car racing looks like a solitary sport: a car and a driver and a track; the skill and courage of a single driver pitted against a field of drivers. But listen to that interview: The driver *never* uses the word "I" when referring to what happens

> *"You'll never get ahead of anyone as long as you try to get even with him."*
>
> *- Lou Holtz*

on the track. "We were running pretty good through the whole first 50 laps," or "We're just trying to run our race,"...you get the idea. Drivers understand that although they may be the "face" of the racing team, it is the *team* that is important. Winston Cup champion Jeff Gordon said it best when he said, "Teamwork is everything. It takes all of us working together. We win and lose together."

In sports as well as in business, highly performing teams are most often the reason organizations are successful. Even superstars recognize they don't get to the championship on their own. Take 2012 Heisman Trophy winner and Texas A&M quarterback Johnny Manziel for example. Watching Manziel play, it's clear to

88

even the novice football fan that he's an incredibly gifted athlete. It would be easy to credit Texas A&M's success during the 2012 season to Manziel's heroics on the field, but Manziel didn't see it that way. Standing on the national stage after becoming the first freshman ever to win one of college football's most prestigious awards for individual achievement, he said,

> *"It's such an honor to represent Texas A&M and my teammates here tonight; I wish they could be on the stage with me."*

The young man known as "Johnny Football" understood that he plays as part of a team and that together the team is stronger than any one player.

I like the quote from G.K. Chesterton at the beginning of the chapter because it's typical of him to wrap up a diamond of insight with some wry humor. Chesterton was right; there is not time or money for one person to learn by trial and error. We have to be able to learn from our teammates and our competitors. Furthermore, individual leaders mentoring younger leaders in the same industry can reap benefits to all by expanding the talent base and bringing in fresh ideas. An industry that doesn't grow its own talent as well as recruit new talent is doomed to extinction through stagnation. I have seen many organizations turn inward and rest on their laurels only to become stale and ineffective. Eventually "stale" becomes "dead."

In any workforce, almost everyone has something to contribute. In my experience, it's a rare condition when someone is *completely* ineffective. As Chesterton says, we don't have time to make all our mistakes ourselves. Being a learning organization, and learning leaders, means we can build a culture of mutual support and teamwork that raises our performance with each experience.

The leaders' challenge is to encourage a healthy partnership with the network of people and organizations they serve, that serve them, and that they compete with. That's what we do at professional organizations and societies, that's what we do when we meet with suppliers and support organizations, and that's even what we do when we celebrate with birthday cake in the conference room.

Teaming With Friends and Competitors

In industry, complex relationships have developed between companies operating in the modern global economy. Alliances between companies are often transient, and different business units in the same company can be teamed with other companies on various projects. It's not uncommon for companies to team with industry competitors and even to compete with other business units internal to their own company.

> *Vertical integration within the industry has generated complex teaming and joint venture relationships that can be characterized with the terms "Coopertition" (a joint-venture between competitors) and "Competemies" (individual business units within the same company competing for the same contract).*[16]

In this sort of an environment, every organization must be constantly looking for teammates. Internal teams are easy to define and manage, but every organization has external teammates as well: our suppliers, colleagues in other departments or business units, even competitors or industry partners. In any line of work, we shouldn't lose sight of the things our external teammates do for us (or *can* do for us). Teamwork is not a platitude or a motivational picture on the wall; it's a way of approaching work.

As a young officer, I missed an opportunity because I didn't recognize a teammate when I saw him. In the early 1990s, the Air

---

16 Colonel Michael Addison (ed), et al, "Spring 2009 Industry Study Final Report, Land Combat Systems Industry," (Masters capstone paper, Industrial College of the Armed Forces, National Defense University, 2009)

Force had adopted Total Quality Management (TQM) as an overarching organizational philosophy. As a result, we began a series of "awareness" classes in TQM theory and practice at each level of command. During an exercise in my week-long introduction to TQM, we were put into a team and given the task to produce paper airplanes. We spent considerable time developing our *internal* processes and then called over the "supplier" (our instructor) to negotiate a price for our raw materials. The goal was to spend the least amount of money and produce the most paper airplanes. We quickly developed an adversarial relationship with our "supplier," who repeatedly stressed that he had plenty of "Grade A" paper for our airplanes. After extracting the best possible deal from our supplier, a deal he assured us he was losing money on, we produced a number of paper airplanes. It was only *after* the exercise was complete that our "supplier" asked us why we didn't ask him about the rest of his product line. "Why would we want anything other than 'Grade A' paper for our airplanes?" we asked. Then he showed us the "Grade B" paper: sheets of paper already folded in half, and he would've sold them to us at half price. That would've saved a lot of work! Then he showed us the "Grade C" paper: already completed paper airplanes. These were the least expensive of all, a third of the cost of "Grade A" paper. We had never asked our "supplier" what else he had, nor had we invited him into our team. We had simply treated him as a resource to be exploited. A teamwork approach could've gotten our little paper airplane manufacturing company a "win" against our real competitors (the other manufacturing teams) and saved us both time and money. Lesson learned!

Professional organizations are very important in this regard. It's not uncommon for business people competing in the same market to share meals and ideas at the monthly luncheons and seminars. Cooperation between competitors serves everyone well, since there is usually more than enough business to go around. By adopting a "cooperate and graduate" style, even competitors can become partners. Clearly, there are practical and legal limits to cooperation between industry competitors, but having limits doesn't imply there should be no cooperation at all.

Take the case of the US Air Force's newest air superiority fighter, the F-22 Raptor. Boeing and Lockheed-Martin teamed to develop and then manufacture the advanced aircraft rather than compete amongst themselves. A second team, Northrup-Grumman and McDonnell-Douglass, also teamed up to compete for the contract. Both teams partnered for several reasons, among them that it spread the risk out among many business units, and a team approach also ensured that components could be manufactured and assembled in as many Congressional districts as possible to shore up support on Capitol Hill. A more cutthroat approach would've been for a single company to make the pitch to the Air Force, and if they won the contract, they'd have eliminated perhaps several major competitors from the market. However, both teams knew the Air Force was concerned with maintaining the aviation industrial base, and developing new technology is also fraught with risks, so both companies elected to "cooperate and graduate" on the F-22 project so they could minimize their risk and maximize the chance of getting the contract. Now, the Air Force got their fighters, had some confidence that the industry will stay healthy, and both companies in the winning team live to fly another day. Together, the teams of Lockheed-Martin and Boeing were more successful than either would've been on their own.

What's more, while a multi-billion dollar contract certainly had the top executives involved in setting the agenda, think of the cooperation and teamwork required *at the first line supervisor level* at both companies. Engineers and program managers had to make hundreds of decisions per day about what information to share and how to achieve their company's leaders' vision while not compromising future projects. Lockheed-Martin and Boeing were allies in the F-22 project, but they were still competing in the same market for other contracts. That kind of teamwork at the lowest levels requires both a commitment to supporting the first line leaders (and "foot soldiers") by headquarters and first line leaders' commitment to protecting their own company's interests at the same time. That kind of "tight rope" only works if first line leaders are given clear guidance and entrusted with the responsibility to get the job done by their leaders. People have to be able to make decisions and not "wait for guidance." The more complex the situation, the more important first line leaders are to the success of an enterprise.

Group Dynamics and the Leader

In 1965 Bruce Tuckman developed what I believe to be one of the best models for understanding group dynamics: "Forming-Storming-Norming-Performing."[17] I like this particular model because I've seen it played out more than once in both my professional career and personal life. This isn't a book about group dynamics, it's a book about leadership; so group dynamics are only interesting to us as it pertains to the leader's role.

In the first phase, "Forming," the group begins to get to know each other, sort out roles, and establish order. The next phase, "Storming," describes the friction between the group members as they come into conflict over their place in the group and the group's purpose. "Storming" is followed by "Norming" as the group establishes patterns and standards for how they'll operate. Finally, in the "Performing" phase, the group is firing on all cylinders. They've worked out their rules, established a managerial

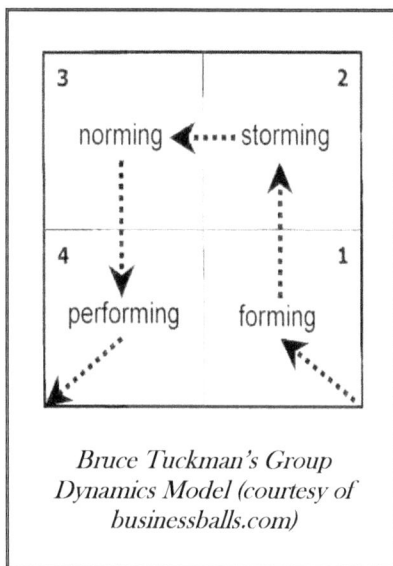

Bruce Tuckman's Group Dynamics Model (courtesy of businessballs.com)

17 Businessballs.com, "Bruce Tuckman's 1965 Forming Storming Norming Performing Team-development Model," accessed 22 Nov 2012.
http://www.businessballs.com/tuckmanformingstormingnormingperforming.htm.

system, and everyone has a role.

Tuckman saw the leader's role was to guide the group through the stages, changing leadership styles as the group matured.[18] In the beginning, the leader would be very directive, and as the group matures, the leadership style would eventually become almost detached. In my mind, the leader's job is to get the team to the "Performing" stage as quickly and smoothly as possible. If the leader has laid the Cornerstone, "Integrity," and the Second Brick, "Respect," then he's already set the conditions for good teamwork. However, even homogenous teams formed around altruistic goals and nice people will *still* "Storm" before they "Perform." Just visit any volunteer organization and you're bound to see it sooner or later.

A friend of mine took on a difficult leadership challenge at a volunteer resale shop where she worked. The volunteer-run organization had all the makings of a wonderful place. The staff members were all local civic minded volunteers, many retired, and all deeply involved in their community. Proceeds went to charity. All the elements for a superbly performing team were present, but the organization was stressed by a change in leadership and policies brought on by financial decisions the organization's oversight board made. When my friend arrived, the organization showed all the signs of Post-traumatic Stress Disorder at the group level.

Despite all the potential for a happy, motivated staff, the volunteers were generally unfulfilled and the atmosphere awkward. As an organization, it was becoming dysfunctional. They disagreed over small concerns and wasted energy on comparisons of what each volunteer was doing rather than progress toward the shared

---

18 Ibid.

goal. To say that the volunteers were stuck in the "Storming" phase of group dynamics would be an understatement. And while the organization raised plenty of money, there was very little sense of mission or accomplishment by the staff.

First line leadership was solid and engaged but they weren't empowered to make many decisions on their own. The senior volunteer, a director, supervised several other volunteer subordinate assistants and was responsible to a volunteer board of directors. Because the same volunteers worked the same shifts all the time, the natural tendency to form cliques meant there was unhealthy competition between groups internal to the

> *Giving teams a sense of mission, particularly with volunteers, is very important. People will give their best when they believe in their cause.*

organization. The nature of the business itself was very fluid, because inventory and customers were rarely the same from day to day. The fluidity of the work required broad guidelines coupled with both volunteers and volunteer leaders making a lot of judgment calls. A casual visitor would never have known that the organization was a charity. The work area was Spartan and rules of conduct fairly rigid. In truth, my friend was in awe of the dedicated volunteers that chose to put up with the drudgery in order to do something good for their community. The whole place had a "pressure cooker" feel, where volunteers were reluctant to make decisions, and most tough decisions were either "kicked down the road" or made at the top level.

My friend took over leadership along with two others of the organization in an advisor/coach role. She quickly made small but important changes to procedures and "atmospherics" in an effort to give the volunteers a sense of mission and purpose. She held a number of meetings with the volunteers to explain the changes she was making and to encourage them that it was OK to take risks and to ask questions. She assured them she wanted *their* input into how things should be run. Many had been volunteering there for years but had rarely been included in decisions on how to operate. At first, my friend was peppered with "What do I do about...?" questions. But with the gentle support of the senior leadership team, the volunteers were encouraged into the "Norming" stage. When they were supported in their decisions, they gained confidence to make more. In time, the rules became the boundaries for getting to the goal—money for charity—rather than a bludgeon to keep the volunteers in line.

She also facilitated significant changes in how the "additional duties" like taking out the trash and organizing the storeroom were done. Instead of these tasks being "assigned," the newfound sense of ownership led the staff to volunteer to do the unpleasant tasks without being told. My friend made a point of praising those that had volunteered, as well as doing some of the more undesirable jobs herself to set the example. When people began to show more ownership in the place itself, others were inspired to join in and contribute as well. Small acts of service to one another among the volunteers moved them to begin to look for other ways to contribute.

The next and probably most important change my friend made was to remind the volunteers why they were there in the first place. She created a newsletter that reminded the staff about the charities they were supporting, with photos of the beneficiaries. She replaced the harshly worded "NO!" signs with "Please" signs. In short, she changed the tone from one that made the volunteers feel like they were doing court-imposed community service to an environment of camaraderie, even family, and *purpose.*

After a year of hard leadership work, the place was already showing a lot of improvement. The volunteers who couldn't or wouldn't adapt moved on, and the long-suffering volunteers who had been enduring the place started participating in the decision making. They even started recruiting new staff. My friend was successful because she knows that real change only occurs when the team understands where they're going, believes they're respected, and has leaders at every level empowered to make decisions.

I had a similar experience leading a group of volunteers when I took over as parish council president in a small suburban parish, only the problem turned out to be me. Our parish priest had asked me to take over as parish council president, and I reluctantly accepted his nomination. After an election, I got the job. Shortly after, however, our pastor was re-assigned without being replaced, and I was left with the de facto leadership of the parish and the council. I hadn't served on a parish council before and didn't appreciate how the job was basically limited to managing the parish finances. In the absence of a permanent pastor, however, I assumed I had leadership of the paid and unpaid staff as well as the council members. Bad assumption, particularly since they knew better. In trying to assert my authority to continue on as I thought our priest had wanted, I made a number of significant mistakes, starting with ending the contract of a musician without speaking to her directly. I had tried unsuccessfully to make contact via telephone, and when my phone calls were unanswered, I simply allowed the contract to expire, expecting the paid secretary to make the follow-up phone calls. Needless to say, by not making contact with a person who was on our payroll *before* terminating the contract, I exposed the parish to embarrassment at best and liability at worse. When I was finally able to make contact (weeks after the contract ended), the musician and her husband were understandably upset. In this case, the burden to make contact was mine, and I failed to ensure it was done properly.

Poor communication was a trend throughout my tenure as president. I had a busy "day job" and tried to delegate responsibility to the various committee heads and volunteers the same way I did at work: email. This method was not very successful as most of my council members didn't even *use* email. Furthermore, I didn't appreciate that I was dealing with volunteers who *also* had day jobs, and so I couldn't fire off tasks to my "staff" and then act disappointed at the meeting when it wasn't done. I learned to be more modest in my expectations and a little less ambitious in how we planned to expand. I also learned that I needed to follow up with a phone call and follow up more than once. Unfortunately, no matter how I tried, I couldn't solve the problem. My last act as parish council president was to apologize to the newly elected president who was nominated but didn't run and had asked me not to put his name on the ballot. A series of assumptions and misunderstandings between me and the volunteers running the election had resulted in a very badly run election that put a man in office who had specifically asked not to be considered. It was very embarrassing for me, the parish council volunteers, and the new pastor. We moved out of town to a new job a few weeks later, so I don't know how the new pastor handled it, but I'm sure he wasn't pleased at being handed a mess on his first day.

The lessons I learned from this particular little exercise in group dynamics is not to take for granted that people operate the same way I do. Furthermore, I learned not to mistake "harmony" for a group that is "Performing." My parish council members all got along famously, but without clear, achievable goals (instead of my grandiose vision), even the simplest tasks became muddled. Instead of trying to manage the group by telephone and email, I really needed to be personally involved in what they were doing. Because of the nature of what we were doing, and because of what our fellow parishioners expected of us, I also needed to exert more control over processes than I did. I should've recognized that having our pastor's office vacant meant that the normal coordination and approval checks that existed when Father was there simply didn't in his absence. As a group, our parish council was stuck in the "Norming" phase of group development. We were clearly not "Performing."

Recognizing & Promoting Excellence

Leaders should deliberately recognize and reward excellence of members as a means of encouraging excellence for both the team as a whole and by individuals. This usually takes the shape of a formal recognition program, but it should also include informal recognition as well. The real trick for the skilled leader is to know how to balance those two forms of recognition.

Formal recognition programs are certainly the most prevalent and can be very effective at promoting excellence if managed carefully. Virtually every organization of any size has an "Employee of the Month" or similar program. These are important; however, I believe the leader must deliberately manage these programs to avoid having them become meaningless. Because they are ubiquitous, there can be a tendency among employees to discount or even make fun of the program. It's really up to the leader to be sure that doesn't become the case by ensuring the process for selecting winners is fair, objective, and non-repetitive. It's very easy for a busy leader to select winners for these sorts of programs randomly or casually. Leaders must resist the temptation to do so. So long as there is a defined process and objective criteria that everyone knows, and the leader *follows* the process, then the team will respond positively to "of the month"

> *Leaders don't have to do recognition all by themselves. Subordinate leaders can assist by prompting the senior leader to recognize employees and keeping up on personal triumphs and tragedies. Remind the junior leaders often to "push up" requests for recognition by seniors.*

programs. However, if the employees see the same people winning time after time, or believe (even erroneously) that winners are selected based on their ability to "butter up" management, then no amount of sincere praise will make the winners feel special and recognized.

I had a personal experience where this derision of the recognition program surprised me greatly. We had a "do it yourself" shop at an Air Force base where I was stationed as the Operations Chief in a public works department. The DIY shop was staffed by a small group of fairly senior people, and they consistently did heroic work to enable the Airmen at various units around the base to fix things themselves instead of waiting for facility maintenance personnel to come do it for them. We saved hundreds of thousands of dollars per year in labor, and the program encouraged pride in the facilities by the Airmen. On top of that, our DIY program was consistently regarded as one of the best of the dozen or so in Air Combat Command. The surprise came, however, when I attempted to recognize the civilian manager who led the DIY shop. He came to my office and emotionally demanded that I remove his name from contention as "Civilian Manager of the Quarter."

While he never gave me a specific reason, I believe he'd lost faith in the process. I think he had come to believe that the selection of winners for the quarterly awards was based only on "favorites" and wanted no part of it. Reluctantly, I agreed not to recognize him, but it gave me impetus to make some significant changes in how we selected our award winners in the future. I made sure the mini-boards for selecting our winners were composed of more people and that the process was more formalized. I also made sure we were keeping notes as to who had won and from which shop, to be sure that we spread the awards around and looked for people who were performing in the "shadows" rather than just "out front." It took a while, but I believe that by the time I'd left, we'd restored a measure of trust in the system.

Informal recognition can also be very effective, if the leader spreads out his time and attention and ensures he really does recognize excellence. A hand-written note, presentation of a challenge coin, a personal word of encouragement during a visit to the work center, or even the presentation of a small cash award are all examples of informal recognition. Sometimes just knowing that the "big boss" knows what an employee has accomplished either at work or in her private life is sufficient to motivate that employee to continued excellence.

> *Team awards can take many forms: peer nominations, on-the-spot, and formal. There's no one formula, so find what works for your organization and go for it!*

People want to be valued, and they enjoy the idea that their leaders have taken a personal interest in their achievements. It makes the employees feel like they're part of a team rather than just a cog in the machine. When I am in leadership positions, I make a point to learn as many names as possible and to learn enough about the people who work for me to relate to them on a personal level rather than just superficial small talk. I still forget from time to time—nobody is perfect—but I believe that people appreciate it when you make the effort. Trying to get to know my team members more deeply than "happy talk" demonstrates that I am doing my best to truly listen when they talk and that I value them as people.

Finally, I believe it's very important to recognize the excellence of *teams* in addition to individual achievement. If the leader wants to encourage teamwork, then recognizing successful teams is a concrete way to do that. Team awards shouldn't replace individual awards, but team recognition has a number of benefits. First, it emphasizes that team success is every bit as important as individual success. Teams are made up of individuals, but a single superstar can't carry a team for very long. Lasting success is often built on individuals pooling their talents to be successful together. A team award recognizes that idea. Second, a team award enables the leader to recognize more people. There will always be someone who could never be "employee of the month" on their own. Their work might be too mundane, or it might be too difficult to quantify in an award nomination. Perhaps a certain person is just not pleasant to be around but consistently produces good work. Or perhaps a person is simply a solid "C+" player that works hard every day with a great attitude but not much aptitude. A team award is an excellent motivational tool for people in that category and recognizes *everyone's* contribution to the team without compromising the integrity of an individual award by a "gift" nomination to said "C+" employee.

Show Initiative, Work Together

Finally, one of the most important traits a leader can cultivate is initiative. If a leader is explaining the endstate fully and resourcing the job properly, then subordinates are in a position to make decisions to reach the goals the leader lays out. Individual initiative is as important in small teams as it is in large ones.

Take the example of a small short order kitchen staff composed of a chef, a sous chef, and a helper/dishwasher. A three-person team is not complex, and short order cooking is not (normally) complex. But when orders are pouring in quickly, the chef has to be sure the other two members of the kitchen understand their roles *and know the others' roles too.* If the chef has done his job properly, then any of the three can back the others up. If that occurs, the team gets a passing grade. If the team is *really* performing at a high level, then each member of the team is looking ahead and anticipating problems for each other. For example, the chef could notice that the supply of thawed meat is getting low and get more out of the freezer. The helper could see orders for asparagus stacking up and wash a new supply so it's ready to cook. You get the idea. Put simply, a "C" team is merely a collection of individuals on a shared task; an "A" team is invested in the team's success by being invested in the success of their teammates. A high performing team doesn't wait for the leader to make a decision; rather, the team members anticipate problems and work together to solve them *before* they become problems.

> *"It is amazing how much can be accomplished if no one cares who gets the credit."*
>
> *- John Wooden*

106

What's more, team members call out danger or pitfalls for their teammates. In Air Force parlance, that's called being a "good wingman." In any form of combat, the wingman is the one charged with protecting the lead. The wingman is the extra pair of eyes and ears, as well as the extra weapon, to keep the lead safe by calling out danger when he sees it and eliminating threats when possible. That's why a successful team has to be composed of people invested in the team's success. If everyone is out for "number one," and if the leader permits backstabbing and self-serving behavior, then the team will crumble as soon as it's stressed. However, if the team works together, then everyone has the chance to succeed when the team succeeds. Certainly, a place where teammates see each other as fellow travelers instead of competitors is a much more pleasant place to work.

Chapter Take-Aways

- Every job has teammates, even when working alone.

- Strive to see suppliers, competitors, and customers as "teammates" rather than "others."

- Networking isn't merely for finding a job; it's also for keeping one.

- Recognize and reward excellence both formally and informally. It's contagious.

- A handwritten note is always more effective than a form letter. Save the typed memos for official correspondence, and hand write recognition notes.

Questions for Discussion

1. Who are your internal teammates?

2. Who are your external teammates?

3. How do you contribute to the success of your team at your workplace?

4. What does your company get right about teamwork? What do they get wrong?

Brick Five: Little Things Matter

Show me a man who cannot bother to do little things and I'll show you a man who cannot be trusted to do big things.

~Lawrence D. Bell

Check Small Things

It doesn't take much introspection to see how, in business and in life, little things add up to big things. How often have we heard about some fatal accident that could've been prevented with one simple change in behavior? Or a chain of unimportant events that, taken individually, don't amount to much but together add up to a death or serious injury?

The examples are legion: a child is killed in the car wreck because he wasn't buckled in, while the mother walks away; the tourists get lost in the city and are robbed because they didn't pay attention to the warning from the concierge; the aircraft crashed because someone signed off on a routine inspection without ensuring the inspection was actually completed.

In his book, *My American Journey,* General Colin Powell included in his "rules"[19] the phrase, "Check Small Things" because he understands that little things add up to big things. Checking small things is not everyone's forte. However, it must be part of the leader's "cross check" because organizational behavior is the leader's responsibility. The leader must set the standard then ensure there's follow through. I do this by checking the little things when I walk through an area I'm responsible for: Are the fuel tanks full? Did we sign the form? Did they spell my name correctly? Every place has a bulletin board, and there are things that are commonly posted regardless of the function or sector a workplace performs. Company policies and announcements, OSHA and EEOC posters, and safety messages are common. I can tell a lot

---

19 *My American Journey*, Powell, 2003, p 613.

Note: My own "Rules" can be found in Appendix 2, along with a brief explanation.

about a workplace just by checking out the bulletin board. I have made it a practice over the years to check work area bulletin boards whenever I'm in the area.

If a workplace's bulletin board has policies signed by the CEO several CEOs ago, EEOC[20] placards dated 1985, or a company policy that's so faded by the sun it's illegible, then it's a good bet the employees (and the leader) are not paying attention to detail. Bulletin boards like that are symptoms of a culture that allows for things to be in disrepair. Whenever I see a place like that, I immediately wonder what else is not getting the workplace's best effort and how much the leader cares about his team. A leader who's engaged, *who pays attention*, can create an organizational culture where the team *pays attention* to what the leader wants them to do. The principle here is simple: People do what the leader *checks*, not necessarily what the leader *expects*.

When I was an executive assistant for a senior Air Force executive, I saw this principle in action many times. My boss would receive hundreds of pages of documents to read each week; many of those documents had very short timelines for review and often had serious fiscal or staffing considerations for the Air Force. My boss made it a point to read as much as he could, paying particular attention to the most relevant sections

> *As a senior leader, I rarely ask questions to which I don't already know the answer. The question often serves to stimulate analysis and focus the discussion on what I'm truly interested in understanding.*

---

20 EEOC = Equal Employment Opportunity Commission

of the document, but he was very careful to be sure that he also read the "back sections" of whatever he was reviewing. In the beginning of his tenure, he made sure he found something to ask a question about in the last few pages of the document. Sometimes he would even find a sentence fragment or typo that needed correction. In relatively short order, the word got out that "Mr. Smith" read everything he was given. By checking small things like spelling or math and asking questions throughout whatever he was given, my boss was able to reinforce an organizational culture where the staff paid attention to detail. This had the result of improving the thoroughness and accuracy of our staff work, which in turn ensured that our senior Air Force leaders were making decisions based on the best possible information and analysis.

Cleanliness Is Next to Godliness

In life, and in business, neatness counts and attention to detail is important, both as an indicator of the quality of the work the team is doing and in the quality of the team members themselves. Poor performance could be because of poor training, perhaps a poor understanding of what the teammate is doing, or maybe a personal problem that needs attention. In any case, the leader can tell a lot by the little things and little things that may require his attention.

Work area cleanliness is sometimes a good indicator whether the staff is organized and motivated. When you walk into a place of business or an office of some sort, no matter what your personality type, you make judgments about the effectiveness and productivity of an organization by what the area looks like. Of course, there are the practical considerations of health and safety, but teammates and customers are certainly judging you by your workspace!

A personal story about workplace cleanliness comes to mind. Back in the 1990s (when computers were much simpler), I did a lot of the work on my own computer; fixing problems and upgrading the hardware was a hobby. Occasionally, there would be a problem I couldn't fix myself, so I had to go to a professional to make the repairs. I was always looking for a bargain repair shop as opposed to taking my machine to one of the "big box" electronic stores for the repairs, which in those days meant small one- or two-person repair shops.

I found a small shop that was recommended by a friend and walked in with my home-built 386sx computer. The shop was a mess, with computers in various states of disassembly amid papers, Coke cans, chip bags, components, and empty boxes. There was no one at the unfinished wooden counter, so I waited for a moment to see if I'd be helped. I was about to leave the shop when the young man working there that day came around the corner and beckoned me back to the counter. Reluctantly, I placed my machine on the counter and explained what was wrong; he looked at me with little interest then handed me a form to fill out. At the bottom of the form was a damage waiver.

"What's this for?" I asked. The bored young man replied that it was a "standard form" and that it covered the company in case they did cosmetic damage to my computer while it was in their shop. "Like what?" I asked. "Oh, like scratches or dents to the case," he added hastily, "but that never happens." I looked around the shop again. It was a disaster area. Making up my mind quickly, I said, "Uh, I don't think so," then gathered my machine up and left.

> *It's a good idea for senior leaders to join into the "office clean up" day. Pitching in is a good chance to get to know your team better and set the example for the team to follow.*

Would the shop personnel have taken care of my property? Perhaps. Maybe it was just a bad day in the shop; maybe the young man who waited on me was tired or had some other personal issue that prevented him from being more customer oriented. The net result of all those "little things," however, was that in the space of just a few minutes I had lost confidence that this shop was capable or qualified. In fact, I was pretty sure they were going to give my computer back to me with scratches and dents. They lost my business because of the little things. Additionally, they not only lost my business, they also lost the business of all the people to whom I subsequently relayed the story. It had nothing to do with their actual professional or technical ability, training, or certifications. It didn't matter to me that they were not the most expensive shop in town or came highly recommended by peers. My negative reviews were based on a single employee and a single policy for the *potential* that my property would not be respected. Is that unreasonable? Was I applying "military" appearance standards inappropriately? Maybe, but my experience taught me that when a person is unwilling to do the little things, like keeping their work area in order, they are probably unwilling to take care in other facets of their work. The "standard form" just put an exclamation point on the matter for me.

By checking small things, it's much more likely that embarrassing errors will be caught before anyone else sees them. Also, by checking small things, it's very likely that when something is needed, it will be ready. No one wants to go to the first aid kit and find it full of out-of-date medications and missing band aids!

In 2000 Air France Flight 4590 crashed on takeoff, killing all aboard. Ultimately, 113 people were killed and a $107 million aircraft was lost because a 17-inch long by 1-inch wide strip of metal on the runway punctured the fuel tank, starting a fire that ultimately caused the Concorde to crash. The investigation later determined that the metal strip that fell from the aircraft that took off just prior to the Concorde, the one that caused the deaths of 113 people, came from an engine of a DC-10 from Houston. The crash investigation determined that the strip of metal was neither manufactured nor installed properly. The inattention of the maintenance crews in Houston, 5,300 miles away, resulted in a disaster in Paris months later.

I know that an aircraft crash is an extreme example—most of us will not fly a $107 million Concorde—but it illustrates how a seemingly small detail can have very big consequences.

Former Notre Dame head football coach, author, and ESPN sportscaster Lou Holtz knows a thing or two about success. Coach Holtz had a win/loss record of 249–132–7 during his coaching career, including a perfect 12–0 record during Notre Dame's 1988 National Championship season. Coach Holtz is a believer that attention to detail is a key to success and once said, "In the successful organization, no detail is too small to escape close attention." Any football coach will affirm that the game often turns on the small things, and while the coach can't play the game for the players, it's the coaching staff that drills and practices the players so that attention to detail becomes their habit. In football, as in life, sometimes success comes to the team that makes the fewest mistakes by keeping track of the little things.

Watch Your Language

Leaders should be very careful what they say, and to whom, or risk someone executing an order that was not given. People are eager to please, especially for a boss they like (or are afraid of!) and will try to anticipate what a leader needs. This leads to a lot of "the boss said," or in my case, "the colonel wants" orders being passed around on behalf of the leader.

When I was the chief of operations for a public works organization, I saw "the boss wants" play out many times, sometimes comically. We worked in an old building, actually a collection of trailers and temporary facilities that had been stitched together with plywood ramps and stairs. Although it looked good on the outside, the place was very rickety and in constant need of repair. Although I tried my best to guard my words carefully, as I exited the building one day with my deputy in tow, I made what I thought was an idle comment about the door sticking. Returning a couple of hours later, there was a three-man crew of carpenters working on the door. I stopped to chat with them and ask what they were doing, but before I could get the words out of my mouth, the crew leader proudly announced that he and his crew would "get this door fixed for you, sir!" Of course, I complimented them on their initiative and professionalism, but I was back in my office before I was able to recall that I'd even made a comment at all. To me it was just a comment on the age and general disrepair of the facility, but to my engineers, it was both a rebuke and a challenge to make things right.

The maxim of being careful what you say to subordinates goes the other way too. If a leader has something specific in mind, then he should communicate that to his subordinates. When I was deployed to Kuwait, many of the vehicles we used were leased from the local dealers. As it happened, the contract was up and we were changing our leased vehicles out from one vendor and replacing them with vehicles from another. My vehicle control officer was a young senior airman, eager to please but relatively inexperienced. It was his responsibility to swap out all the vehicles and ensure the right vehicles got to the right parts of the unit. It was winter at the time, and the temperatures were moderate. As both squadron and emergency response force commander, I rated an SUV in order to respond to emergencies both on and off pavement. Before the swap, I had a tan Toyota Forerunner, so as I handed my keys over, I didn't think it was necessary to specify what sort of vehicle I needed. He asked me if there was anything in particular I wanted, or a particular color I preferred, and not wanting to seem like I was exerting privilege, I told him to use his best judgment. Eager to please, my young Airman headed out to "get the commander a new vehicle." He was gone all day, and when he returned, he excitedly told me that he'd "gotten me a really cool vehicle" and beckoned me out to see it. On the way out from my office, he proudly told me how he'd held out for the best pick for me and had spent time getting it clean and ready. He'd even transferred my equipment from my old vehicle.

Emerging from the building he moved aside to show me: a black SUV. "It's a *black* one! Cool, huh?!" he exclaimed proudly. It took me a few seconds to take it all in: a black car, in a place where the summer temps reach 125 degrees Fahrenheit. To say that I was not enthusiastic about driving around in a black vehicle in the deserts of Kuwait would be an understatement. But I didn't dare let this nice young man know that. I had given him the freedom to pick the color of my vehicle, and he had exercised that freedom to choose a black one. All I could do was smile and shake his hand to thank him for taking so much care with my vehicle. If I had gotten upset or angry, I would have taught that Airman not to take risks, not to make choices. I would not have been growing a leader; I'd have been stunting one instead. When leading more inexperienced people, sometimes the leader has to be willing to accept less than optimum results, even personal discomfort, in order to encourage those people to grow.

Handle Personal Matters Personally

In my own experience as a leader, I have often been surprised at how much impact little things have on people. Each year former and current students from my alma mater, Texas A&M, gather together on the anniversary of the Battle of San Jacinto to commemorate fellow Aggies who have died during the year. Aggies have been gathering at Muster ceremonies around the world each year since 1922. When I was a young officer on the Pacific Air Force's staff in Hawaii, I was the chairman of our local Texas A&M Association of Former Students' Muster Committee. As it happened, General Pat Gamble, the commanding general, was also a Texas Aggie ('67), so we invited him to attend Muster. He was able to come by for a few minutes before heading off to an official function. Our guest speaker that night was another Aggie, Mr. Don Powell ('56), a famous cartoonist who contributed to the Texas A&M school newspaper for a generation. Mr. Powell was the author of a cartoon entitled "dp" that depicted a lovable cadet and his sidekick. It was a cherished memory of days gone by, especially if you were an Aggie sports fan like me. As souvenirs for the evening, Mr. Powell signed copies of his cartoons, so I asked him to sign a "dp" cartoon for General Gamble. Mr. Powell graciously obliged.

The next day at work, I quickly typed up a short note thanking the general for coming to Aggie Muster, attached the signed cartoon, and delivered it to the general's secretary. I didn't expect to hear from the general again; after all, he commanded a vast organization responsible for protecting the airspace across the entire Pacific Ocean with thousands of Airmen and hundreds of airplanes, and I was a mere captain. But sure enough, in a day or two I received a handwritten note card with a thank you from the general. That act of kindness—and good manners—made a big impression on me. That handwritten note probably took General Gamble a couple of minutes to write. He likely forgot about it as soon as he'd done it, but to this day that note is the reason I still don't sign form "letters of appreciation" prepared by my staff. Countless members of my own units have received handwritten notes all because years ago a very busy man took a couple minutes to write a personal note to me.

I have come to believe in the power of the personal touch when leaders interact with their teams. People may *say* they don't care about what their leaders think about them, but my experience tells me the opposite. It matters when a leader takes the time to personally recognize excellence and when the leader shows interest in the team members' families and personal lives. Certainly there is a line that one shouldn't cross, like dating subordinates or asking uninvited personal questions about family, faith, or politics, but treating people like people who have their own interests and relationships instead of cogs in the machine means leaders should handle some things personally.

Attention to Detail

Many successful professional and collegiate football coaches are renowned for their attention to detail. In fact, many attribute their success to thorough preparation and attention to detail. The coach may call the plays and direct the pre-game training, but once the game begins, success or failure is entirely up to the players executing what they've learned and practiced. It takes discipline to get all 11 players working together, and not only working together, but executing the plays when they're hot, or tired, or under pressure. That discipline, so prized by football coaches and players, is a key to success in the game. It's why the athletes drill plays over and over; it's why coaches spend hours reviewing films of their opponents; and it's why attention to detail is so prized by those who play and coach the game.

Bill Snyder, the head football coach at Kansas State, is legendary for his attention to the little things. He took over a struggling football program in 1988 to lead one of the most successful college football programs in the country. Snyder's 159 wins make him the 11th winningest active coach in the NCAA Football Bowl Series. He won the 2011 Woody Hayes and *The Sporting News* Coach of the Year awards, and was a four-time winner of Coach of the Year honors from the Big Eight Conference. Coach Snyder's leadership of his players extends off the field as well. The Kansas State football program has the number one graduation rate in the Big XII Conference at 71%.

Bob Stoops, University of Oklahoma head coach and former Snyder assistant, said of his mentor (emphasis mine),

> *"It's hard to say one thing when you're around a guy for 10 years playing and coaching and then seven years as a coach for him, I think attention to detail, **all the***

little things matter; evaluation and developing your team and being methodical and constant about it.[21]

Snyder himself attributes his success to his 16 Rules[22] and hard work, a work ethic learned at a young age and honed during years of making boys into men on the football field. Two of Snyder's Rules relate directly to paying attention to the little things: "Goal 4: Improve" and "Goal 6: Self-Discipline." He has thorough meetings with his assistant coaches and then expects they'll do the same with their players. He requires his players to go to class and stay out of trouble, and he models the self-discipline he requires of his staff and players. Bill Snyder's work ethic is famous, reportedly only sleeping three to four hours a night and eating just one meal a day. Of attention to detail, Snyder says: *"If you do pay attention to detail and the 'little things' are important to you, you make them important to people."*[23] Snyder has reportedly paid attention to things as small as what sort of butter his players get and subtle changes in opponents' formations.

At age 73 and on his second "tour" as head coach of the Kansas State Wildcats, Coach Snyder is still going strong. At the end of the 2012 season, his 11–1 Wildcats were Big XII Champions again and played in the Fiesta Bowl. His quarterback was a 2012 Heisman Trophy contender. The impact Snyder has had on big time football is immense: His former assistants and

---

21 NewsOn6.com. "Bob Stoops Full of Genuine Respect for His Mentor Bill Snyder," 20 Sep 12, accessed 6 Dec 12, http://www.newson6.com/story/19598768/bob-stoops-full-of-genuine-respect-for-his-mentor-bill-snyder.

22 "Bill Snyder 16 Goals For Success List: Kansas State Coach's Thesis Lifted Team To 2013 Fiesta Bowl," John Marshall, 2 Jan 13, accessed 9 Mar 13 http://www.huffingtonpost.com/2013/01/03/bill-snyder-16-goals-success-list-kansas-state_n_2394794.html.

23 Andrew Bagnato, ESPN College Football Encyclopedia, "The Curious Cult of College Coaches," accessed 6 Dec 2012, http://sports.espn.go.com/ncf/story?id=2179611.

players are scattered throughout the country in successful programs of their own. His former coaches and players have taken Coach Snyder's method with them, including his legendary attention to detail.

Most leaders don't have to give attention to detail at the same intensity as Bill Snyder, but thorough preparation is a virtue in any line of work. Simple proof-reading of a report or a run-through on a presentation can make the difference between winning and losing a contract. Ensuring the safety lines are painted correctly on the shop floor can prevent serious injury. Clearly, there's a fine line between the sort of attention to detail by a leader that inspires college football players to win games and the sort that inspires employees to run for the door, but in any case, it's important for the leader to "walk the talk." That's really the main difference between a tyrant and an inspirational leader: his willingness to do the same things he is asking his people to do.

Chapter Take-Aways

- Seemingly insignificant details can have enormous consequences. The leader should understand which details are important and which are extraneous.

- Customers and partners often make sweeping decisions about competence based on a few small details: Ensure your workplace is professional and clean.

- Employees who are allowed to "slack" on little things like workplace cleanliness or "administrivia" are being trained to ignore detail. Murphy's Law dictates that employees will make a big mistake when you can least afford it.

- Successful leaders pay attention to details, and details are often "leading indicators" for organizational performance.

- A leader who's engaged—who pays attention—can create an organizational culture where the team pays attention to what the leader wants them to do.

Questions for Discussion

1. Which details are most important to you in your business? Why?

2. How do you reward attention to detail in your organization? Is it effective?

3. What details do your employees value? Why do you think they value these?

4. How do you communicate which details are important to you, to your suppliers, and to your customers? Are they different sets for different audiences? Why or why not?

Conclusion

Ultimately, leadership is both highly personal and highly situational. There are all sorts of teams and leaders, and the themes and truisms I lay out in this book are universal; each leader has to adapt their own style and personal ethos. I submit that the personal ethos is the first thing a serious leader should reflect on when he takes on a new leadership role. No matter how long a job lasts, be it days or years, the leader should constantly review her ethos in light of the task at hand. My ethos, the philosophy outlined in this book, is the man I want to be when I lead and the values I want my organization to manifest.

As an instructor at the Air Force Officer Training School (OTS), I saw the officer trainees take on the personality of their leaders time and time again. Each of us flight commanders were different in our approach to instruction. One thought of OTS as "adult education," while another acted as if he'd just come off the set of Stanley Kubrick's *Full Metal Jacket.* Each of the groups of officer trainees soon adopted the personality traits of their leader. The transformation was dramatic in some cases, and the military training environment intensified it. For me, it underscored my need to be sure I was the sort of leader I wanted people to emulate, because I knew they'd be taking my example as well as my instruction out into the Air Force.

I believe, if a leader is truly successful, you tell in the demeanor and character of the people he leads. It's often surprising to me how much organizations, even large ones, take on the personality of the leader. It's incumbent, therefore, on the leader to be a person of character, because he has great influence on the character of others. Once a leader understands that essential mandate—truly gets it—he is never the same person again. **Integrity** must be our watchword, because, without it, we cannot hope to build teams that trust each other. **Respect** is the common ground teammates join on to accomplish their professional and personal goals. **Leaders Lead** when they take charge and motivate others to achieve and grow. **Teamwork** is essential to reaching any end; individual achievement is almost always the result of shared effort. Finally, a leader's strict attention to detail means that he fully understands the task and which **Little Things Matter** to getting things done. These are basic ideas, but without these principles as a solid foundation, a leader is without a starting place.

Before the satellite navigation, Global Positioning System, the most advanced navigation system was called the Inertial Navigation System (INS). In order to navigate from place to place, an INS device had to know precisely where it was at the start. Knowing that, the machine used speed and time to calculate distance and precise location along the route. The device was even used to navigate to the moon and back during the Apollo missions.

Like the fixed starting point for the INS, the principles described in this book are the starting point: a precise location to launch from for any leadership journey. If your personal leadership ethos is based on character, you'll have a solid foundation no matter whether you're leading a Boy Scout troop, a small business or major corporation, or battalions in combat.

About the Author

Colonel Mickey Addison is an Air Force officer, author, speaker, husband, and father. He commanded three engineer squadrons and a support group. Mickey has served in staff positions at Headquarters Pacific Air Forces, Headquarters, US Air Force, and Office of the Secretary of Defense. In 1992 he was competitively selected as an instructor at the Air Force Officer Training School, where he was the top graduate from their instructor qualification course.

From 2002 to 2003 he commanded the 332d Expeditionary Civil Engineer Squadron, Ahmed Al Jaber Air Base, Kuwait, during the conclusion of Operation Southern Watch and the initial phases of Operation Iraqi Freedom. From 2011–2013, Mickey commanded the 10th Mission Support Group at the US Air Force Academy and was responsible for more than 1,900 Airmen and civilians, providing all logistics, recreation, personnel, acquisition, and emergency services for a military community of more than 25,000 service members, families, and retirees.

Mickey holds bachelors and masters degrees in engineering (Texas A&M and University of Texas – San Antonio) and two masters degrees in national & public policy formulation (Air University & National Defense University).

His military decorations include the Defense Superior Service medal, the Legion of Merit, the Bronze Star, and numerous other Air Force decorations. He is a 2009 Distinguished Graduate from Industrial College of the Armed Forces.

He's married, and he and his wife, Betsy, have two children, Luke and Haley.

This is Mickey's third book with Blue Mantle Publishing.

For Further Reading

Master Your World, Mary Kelly

Lorenz on Leadership: Lessons on Effectively Leading People, Teams and Organizations, Stephen R. Lorenz

The Courage to Succeed, Ruben Gonzalez

Getting to Yes: Negotiating Agreement Without Giving In, Roger Fisher, William L. Ury, and Bruce Patton

Good to Great, Jim Collins

Rules & Tools for Leaders, Perry M. Smith

Leaders and Battles: The Art of Military Leadership, W. J. Wood

George Washington on Leadership, Richard Brookhiser

Leadership Lessons of Robert E. Lee, Bil Holton

Decision Points, George W. Bush

Last Chance for Victory: Robert E. Lee and the Gettysburg Campaign, Scott Bowden and Bill Ward

Tom Landry: An Autobiography, Tom Landry

Winning Every Day: The Game Plan for Success, Lou Holtz

The Art of the Handwritten Note, Margaret Shepherd

Defense of Hill 781: An Allegory of Modern Mechanized Combat, James R. McDonough

The Heart of Change, John P. Kotter

Not a Good Day to Die: The Untold Story of Operation Anaconda, Sean Naylor

The Lost Peace: Leadership in a Time of Horror and Hope, 1945-1953, Robert Dallek

Secrets of Special Ops Leadership: Dare the Impossible—Achieve the Extraordinary, William Allen Cohen

Appendix 1 – Mickey's Rules

For years I kept General Colin Powell's "Rules" on a worn, type-written sheet of paper somewhere on my desk. His Rules had been published in a news magazine article, and I thought they were fabulous, so I typed them up and added a few of my own to the bottom. Over the years, I developed my own "Rules" that gradually replaced "Colin Powell's Rules" even though that worn piece of paper still adorns my desk.

I've found these rules to be very useful to me, and I've regretted it every time I've violated them. The eleven rules listed on the next page are my guidelines for relating to other people and to my work and reminders about leading my organization. This list will be the subject of another book, so if the phrases are a bit cryptic, be patient!

Mickey's Rules

1. Have a direction and know what it is. Go there.
2. Don't spook the herd. Emotional demonstrations are always counter-productive and stifle initiative.
3. Don't let "perfect" be the enemy of "good."
4. "Can't" never gets anything done. Keep it out of your vocabulary.
5. The first report is usually wrong. Be patient and ask questions.
6. Asking the right questions is usually better than knowing the right answers.
7. The other team is not the enemy. The enemy is the enemy; don't confuse the two.
8. Be curious. Ask "Why?" a lot. Keep asking until you understand.
9. Walk the horses. No one can go full throttle all the time.
10. Drink your water, eat your lunch, and make new friends.
11. Check your "moral azimuth"...if you're doing something that you wouldn't want posted on the Internet, it's probably illegal, immoral, or fattening.

Appendix 2
Sample Employee & Team Feedback Form

Name:	Dept/Team:	Position:	Feedback Date:
Primary Duties & Responsibilities:			

	Sets the Standard	Meets Expectations	Needs Improvement
Shows Personal Initiative			
Communicates Clearly			
Dress & Appearance			
Models & Promotes Teamwork			
Recognizes & Promotes Excellence			
Demonstrates Respect for Peers & Subordinates			
Attention to Detail			

Appendix 3 – Developing Your Leaders' Ethos

1. Write three core values that define who you are:

----

2. How do you best communicate with subordinates?

----

3. How do you best communicate with your boss?

----

4. Who are your customers?

----

5. What is the most important characteristic of your organization's product or service?

_____

_____

_____

6. In ten words or less, write a sentence that describes the type of person you'd like to be.

_____

_____

_____

7. Describe your "top 3" pet peeves:

_____

_____

_____

Order Form

Email Address: _____

Daytime Phone: _____

Billing Address

Name: _____

Street Address: _____

City / State / Zip: _____

Country: _____

Shipping Address (if different than Billing Address)

Name: _____

Street Address: _____

City / State / Zip: _____

Country: _____

Payment Information:

Qty: _____ x $19.95 = _____

Plus Shipping @$2.50/book = _____

TOTAL = _____

Credit Card: MC/Visa Number: _____

Exp: _____ Security Code: _____

Scan and email to: michael.a.addison@gmail.com

www.mickeyaddison.com

Leading Leaders is available at Lulu.com in paperback, hardback, or ebook formats. A workbook also available!

Just point your browser to:

http://www.lulu.com/spotlight/mickeyaddison

to order!